TEN

MORE

ADVENTUROUS WALKS IN

SURREY

Raymond Hugh

Illustrations by
Jackie Hei

ISBN 1 874476 04 7

Published by Morning Mist Publications 1993
PO Box 108, Reigate, Surrey RH2 9YP
©Raymond Hugh & Jackie Hei 1993

Designed and Printed by
Advanced Data Graphics, Sevenoaks

INDEX

INTRODUCTION

AN APOLOGY

Most of the adventures described in this book tread new ground and uncover new secrets. On occasion however, mainly as a result of an area being of particular outstanding beauty, a route will cross or meet that of the original book, "10 Adventurous Walks in Surrey", or visit the same village. If you have purchased the original book, I apologise that the historical interest notes, unless something spectacular has happened in the last year, remain the same. Happily however, this happens only rarely and I therefore believe you will find the new walks offer a completely different set of adventures.

If you are not the proud owner of the original Surrey book, then - **why not?!**

THE ADVENTURE

The adventure must be yours, it is the thrill of exploration, the pleasure of experiencing something new and the surprise of the unexpected. You could do the same walk several times and each time it will be different. You will often surprise some of the many rabbits which graze and feed off the slopes of the famous North Downs and on occasions, you may be lucky enough to spot a hungry kestrel hovering above its next kill. On a summer's day the chalk downs are alive with the colour and bustle of busy bees and insects visiting the chalkland flowers. In winter, this is replaced by the mournfall swaying of trees in the wind and the swift movement of wildlife, no longer protected by the leafy foliage of warmer months. The weather can change not only the appearance of a walk, but also the feel. The adventure is discovering the secrets of the route on the day.

THE REWARD

The reward is the sense of achievement and the knowledge that not only have you completed a respectable distance, you will have learned and experienced something of Surrey which before was a mystery. There is no greater satisfaction than to discover the county as our ancestors did - on foot.

WHEN TO GO

Many walkers make the mistake of only walking in fine weather, leaving the hills at the slightest sign of rain. In wet and windy weather the countryside is untamed and with the majority of the population safe in their houses, one can really get a feeling of remoteness and a better idea of what Surrey was like several hundred years ago. My suggestion is that you try and do the walks in all seasons and all weathers. At the end if you don't hate me, you will really begin to feel an affinity with the Surrey countryside and have the satisfaction of knowing the county well. As for the time of day, I recommend that you try and time your walk to include either dawn or dusk. These to me are the best part of the day, unfortunately, often missed by the majority.

PREPARATION

Planning the walk is as important and enjoyable as doing the walk itself. Firstly, consider whether you want to make a weekend of it. If you do, then I suggest you book local accommodation. This not only cuts down on travelling on the day, but creates a seemingly longer weekend and allows you to remain familiar with the area at night. There is nothing better in my mind than to finish a long walk and retire to local accommodation for a hot bath before a well earned visit to the local village pub, without having to worry about driving home. A selection of recommended accommodation is listed at the end of each walk.

Once you have decided on your walk, familiarise yourself with it. Read the walk through, following it on the map and ensure you understand where it is you are going. The route descriptions contain points of interest and you may want to take time to stop and visit these. If you do, it might be worth borrowing a book from the Library to read up before your visit. Equally, when you have made up your mind on the points of interest to visit, try and estimate the length of your walk. The timings given on each walk are meant as a rough guide only and are based on a person being reasonably fit. If you are unsure, then I suggest you allow for approximately two miles per hour. Timing is important as you could find yourself stumbling back to the start in the dark.

Finally, make sure you are fit. The walks in this book are longer than the average walking book and can be hard work if you are unprepared. To help identify the gradients, a cross section is included at the start of each walk.

WHAT TO TAKE

A good map is essential. I recommend you use the Ordnance Survey Landranger maps and the start of each walk details the map(s) required. You can also use the Ordnance Survey Pathfinder maps which have far more detail such as field boundaries, but they can be harder to find and can ultimately be more expensive.

Once armed with your map, make sure you have sensible clothing. This means clothes which are loose and comfortable. Tight jeans and high heels are not recommended! No matter how good the weather is at the start of the day, always pack some waterproofs. Being caught out in the rain without the necessary protection is not an experience I would recommend. In summer if you are walking in shorts, waterproof trousers are also particularly useful as a temporary protection against nettles. There is a wide range of waterproof clothing now available. The two recommendations I would make are:-

(1) Make sure you are completely covered, that is buy trousers and a jacket.

(2) Buy clothing made from one of the breathable materials - your local stockist will advise you on these.

If the weather is cold, then gloves and a hat are always advisable. No matter what time of year, I always pack a jumper and have never regretted it. Keeping warms helps avoid tiredness. Most importantly, make sure you have a good pair of shoes. If you can afford it, then buy a pair of walking boots. If not, then make sure your shoes are strong, comfortable and have soles with a good grip. Equally important are good socks. If you have boots then two pairs are advisable. Do not think that the socks you wear to the office will do!

Sensibly clothed, you can now think about other equipment you may need. A camera and a pair of binoculars are always useful and can enhance your day out. I always carry a pocket book on birds, you could do the same or add to this with a book on local flora or history. You will find the walk all the more enjoyable for a little bit of knowledge. Do not though, get over enthusiastic and take a library or you may find yourself requiring a book on first aid!

A basic first aid kit however, is always advisable. The Surrey countryside may appear tame and so it is compared to the Himalayas, but it must still be treated with respect, though a compass is always useful for finding your way when paths are undefined.

Refreshments are always an important consideration. There are places where you can get a bite to eat on every walk, but even if you wish to use these facilities, it is important to carry some basic snacks, especially in cold weather. You should always carry water and a thermos flask with a hot drink or soup can also be very welcome.

To carry everything you need for your walk, I recommend you invest in a comfortable day sack or small rucksack. These are now available from a wide assortment of shops, but before you make your purchase, make sure it is strong and more importantly, that it is comfortable.

Finally, take your five senses with you - these are essential if you are to fully appreciate the walk but, most importantly, **ENSURE YOU TAKE THIS BOOK!**

GETTING THERE

Most people will be mobile, i.e. a car or bicycle. Where practical, I have listed railway stations. Buses however, are far more difficult as their routes and timetables tend to change with the wind. For those people relying on a bus to reach the start, I have listed the main bus companies serving the area.

London & Country (Tel: 081 668 7268)

Minicruisers (Tel: 0342 844422)

Taxibus (Tel: 0306 884937)

Tillingbourne (Tel: 0483 276880)

W&H Motors Ltd (Tel: 0293 510220)

Surrey County Council, in conjunction with the Surrey Hills Visitor Project, have recently introduced a number of new services geared to transporting the visitor at weekends to the more remote spots in the Surrey hills. As an added interest, these services use vintage buses from the 1950's and 1960's. Timetables and full details can be obtained from Tourist Offices or by writing to The Passenger Transport Group, Highways & Transportation Dept., Surrey County Council, County Hall, Kingston Upon Thames, KT1 2DY.

For information on rail services, telephone Network South East on - 0732 770111 or 0483 755905.

ROUTE FINDING

The route descriptions are instructional rather than poetic and should be followed without difficulty. To assist you, a series of symbols in the left hand margin enable you to identify specific points on the walk at a glance. A good map is essential and should be used in conjunction with the route description. Please remember that like everything else, the countryside changes with time, e.g. a fenced path can become unfenced and vice versa.

Before setting out, make sure you have identified the route on the map. To pinpoint a starting point or place of interest and key points on the route, I have used grid references which are printed in bold in the text. These are six figured numbers which identify a particular point on the map. Every Ordnance Survey map is covered by a national grid. The grid's lines are identified by numbers printed on the map's surround. To find a grid reference, take the first three numbers, which refer to the vertical lines on your map and locate them on the top or bottom (north or south) of the map. The third number is an imaginary line in the square following the first two numbers. To find this line, divide the square into ten equal parts. Then take the last three numbers, which refer to the horizontal lines and locate them on the left or right (east or west) of your map and follow the line of this reference until it meets the line of the first reference. Their meeting point is the grid reference point itself. Do not rely on the maps in this book, these are not to scale and are meant as a rough guide only.

It is important that you recognise the various types of footpath signs. Most are fairly obvious, i.e. wooden post with a sign marked "footpath" or "public bridleway", pointing in the direction of the right of way. Some will have the name of a specific route, for example, "The North Downs Way".

Over recent years many County Councils have standardised their signs to follow national guidelines. Footpaths are now shown with a yellow arrow and bridleways with a blue one. Like the old wooden signs, the arrows will point in the direction of the right of way. Some arrows will have the initials of a recognised walk imprinted,

the most common one you will see is "GW" which marks the Greensand Way. On top of all this, you will often find custom built signs. These can mark an official route, but more often than not, are the work of local farmers guiding the walker across their land. An example of the former is "The North Downs Way", which is highlighted by a white acorn on a black background.

An important rule on route finding is to take your time. Follow the map and read the route description thoroughly. If you do this, then you will return to base without mishap.

LONG DISTANCE WALKS

Many of the routes in this book meet long distance linear walks which run through Surrey. In case you want to try any, I have listed their names and distances below, together with the publisher who produces a description of the walk.

Downs Link - 30 miles (West Sussex County Council)

Greensand Way - 106 miles (Ramblers Association)

London Country Way - 205 miles (Constable)

North Downs Way - 141 miles (HMSO)

Sussex Border Path - 150 miles (Ben Perkins)

Vanguard Way - 63 miles (Ramblers Association)

Wey South Path - 23 miles (The Wey and Arun Canal Trust)

TOURIST INFORMATION CENTRES

If you require any further information on transport, tourist facilities or accommodation, I have listed the local Tourist Information Centres below.

Farnham - (Tel: 0252 715109)

Guildford - (Tel: 0483 444007)

AUTHOR'S NOTE

Every effort has been made to ensure that the route descriptions are accurate. Time changes things however and can alter the description of the route. If you have any difficulty in finding any part of a route, please write with details giving a grid reference, to enable me to re-examine the route. A free copy of the next publication will be forwarded for any suggestions used in the next edition. Enjoy your walks.

IN SEARCH OF LOST CASTLES

Distance: 8 ¼ miles (13.25 km)
Time: Allow approximately 4 1/2 hours
Map: Ordnance Survey Landranger Map 187

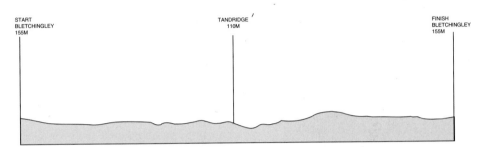

Walk Summary

This walk is ideal as an introduction to this book as the going throughout is fairly easy. Apart from some pretty countryside and glorious views, you will also pass through three extremely attractive villages. Better still are the wide choice of excellent hostelries encountered en route. The only downside is the mud. Many of the paths followed are "boggy", even in dry weather, so make sure you wear those boots!

Start - OS. 326508 Map 187

The walk starts from the war memorial which is on the northern side of the High Street at Bletchingley. Getting there by car is easy as Bletchingley High Street is also the A25. It is fairly easy to park in the High Street though, as ever, please respect the locals' privacy and access.

The nearest railway station is at South Nutfield and from there it is approximately a one and a half mile walk along footpaths and the Greensand Way to join our route at Castle Hill, Bletchingley.

Alternative starts can be made from either Godstone or Tandridge, though parking in these villages is not so easy.

IN SEARCH OF LOST CASTLES

To start the walk, make your way to the war memorial beside the Post Office on the northern side of the High Street. You are now standing in one of the broadest and in my opinion, the most attractive High Street in Surrey, spoilt only by the number of cars that use it. Bletchingley was obviously once a very wealthy village and has a past which I believe is worth discovering before we start.

Bletchingley (OS. 326508 Map 187) *shot to prominence shortly after the Norman conquest when it was given as a reward to Richard de Tonbridge. Richard was head of the powerful de Clare family who took their name from their main stronghold, Castle Clare in Suffolk. Apart from being head of the de Clare's, Richard was also one of the most powerful men in the country and one of the biggest landowners, holding thirtyeight manors in Surrey alone. It is believed that it was Richard who started the construction of a castle (one of the lost castles), at the western end of Bletchingley High Street. It dominated the village until 1264 when it was destroyed, though this is another story and one to be told later. The de Clare's held Bletchingley for eight generations until 1314, when the last male heir was killed at the Battle of Bannockburn in Scotland.*

During the time of the castle, Bletchingley became a market town serving the garrison and the numerous visitors to the baron's fortress. This explains the wide High Street. After the destruction of the castle, Bletchingley failed to win a Royal licence for its unofficial market and with no more passing trade, the market ceased to exist. Bletchingley however, continued to be the seat of some powerful people. After the de Clare's came the Staffords, who built a grand palace to replace the ruined castle at the northern side of the village. The palace was later pulled down by Lord Peterborough in the 17th century, though for some reason he left the gatehouse. This can still be seen today (situated in Brewer Street) and is now a private house. It is a magnificent half timbered building and one of the most impressive in Surrey. One can only begin to imagine the size and splendour of the building it served.

The Staffords' hold on the manor ended in the 16th century with the execution of the third Duke of Buckingham, who was Lord High Constable under Henry VIII. Before this, another member of the family, the first Duke of Buckingham, had been executed on the orders of Richard III. The palace could not have been a very lucky place for its next resident, Sir Nicholas Carew, was also executed. After this, the palace became home to Anne of Cleves who, at the time, must have seemed a dead cert to follow in the footsteps of the palace's previous inhabitants. After Anne of Cleves came Sir Thomas Cawarden, Master of the Revels and Keeper of the King's hunting stores. It is said that, Sir Thomas' unofficial role was Court spy for Henry VIII, which included keeping an eye on several of his wives. Consequently, Sir Thomas became a close consort to Henry and entertained him on more than one occasion at Bletchingley.

After the death of Henry VIII, Sir Thomas was to suffer. He was suspected by Mary of being a protestant and of plotting to bring Queen Jane to the throne. As a result, he was arrested and the palace was searched. Inside a considerable arsenal was discovered, including sixteen cannons, one hundred pikes, one hundred bows and eightysix horsemens' staves. Sir Thomas protested his innocence asking, "Might not an English gentleman keep armour in his country house if he pleased to do so?". He was released but the weapons stayed at the Tower of London where they remained even after Elizabeth I came to the throne.

Another famous Bletchingley inhabitant, in more recent years, was Lord Palmerston. Bletchingley, like Gatton (see "In Pilgrims' Footsteps"), was infamous as a rotten borough, sending two M.P.'s to Parliament, Lord Palmerston being one of the last. At Gatton an urn has an inscription which attempted to bring respectability to the mock elections. At Bletchingley, one M.P., Sir Robert Clayton, who owned the village, resorted to a much more basic tactic. On election day he instructed all the pubs to bring their barrels into the street and made ale free for the day. Although at the time, Bletchingley had only twelve eligible voters to elect two M.P.'s, the turnout was huge with everybody praising the rotten borough system. Although this practice was short lived, a tradition was started and "The Whyte Harte" from 1773 onwards staged Parliamentary elections. Master of respectability, the writer Cobbett, condemned Bletchingley in his usual venomous style calling it, "the vile rotten borough" and went on to observe from a more respectable village, "happily for Godstone out of sight".

Today, Bletchingley has regained its respectable face. Its market may have closed centuries ago but the village still thrives, many of its charming tile hung houses being home to the antique trade and a successful Rolls Royce garage which operates at the eastern end of the High Street. For the walker Bletchingley still retains a good number of hostelries. In the High Street there is "The Whyte Harte Hotel", first mentioned in 1388. For the best food in the village, in my opinion, there is "The Prince Albert", Friary Meux, (also in the High Street). It has a cosy interior made up of several rooms, one of which is a restaurant and out back there is a pleasant garden. The landlord is obviously a car enthusiast and engine parts form a major part of the decoration. At the western end of the High Street, as it leads into Castle Street, is "The Red Lion", Greene King. It may not look it, but this is the village's oldest pub dating from 1309. If you choose to drink here, you will follow in the footsteps of good company as Henry VIII, Catherine of Aragon and Cardinal Wolsey were all once visitors. Another pub worth visiting, if you have time, is the "William IV", Charrington, which is on Little Common Lane. Both "The Red Lion" and the "William IV" serve food. If you prefer to eat en route, then the village Post Office doubles as a general store.

From the war memorial take a tarmac path which runs behind the Post Office and between some beautiful cottages. This is Church Walk, where the houses on the left once formed the original line of the High Street. The ones on the right were built after the market ended and the space was no longer needed. Soon the parish church of St. Mary the Virgin will come into view on your left and you should continue until you reach the gate to the churchyard. Pass through the gate into the churchyard and immediately upon entering, (unless you wish to visit the church), leave the brick path which leads to the church entrance and take a tarmac path right instead.

The Church of St. Mary the Virgin (OS. 327509 Map 187) *dates from the 11th century and still retains its Norman tower. Inside, there is a huge memorial to Sir Robert Clayton, one time owner of Bletchingley and Lord Mayor of London. Of all Sir Robert's attributes modesty certainly wasn't one of them, as he designed the memorial himself!*

The tarmac path takes you to the perimeter of the churchyard where you should pass through a wooden gate to reach a lane, opposite "Court Lodge Farm". Turn left along the lane and follow it past a new housing estate, Clerks Croft and just after the entrance to the housing estate, look out for a footpath on the right which you should take. This, initially goes up a bank to continue along the right hand side of a car park belonging to a newly built Golf Club. The next stage of the walk traverses the golf course, where the directions at times may seem complicated, but the path is well signposted and therefore, easy to follow. To start, after approximately twenty metres, turn left to go across the centre of the car park, in the direction of the public footpath sign, and at the far side bear gently diagonally right, still following the footpath signs. After a further twenty metres, bear left again in the direction of another footpath sign to follow a wide grass track, running between fruit trees.

As the fruit trees end, go over a crossing track and pass through a gap in a hedge ahead, to immediately go over another crossing track and carry straight on. You should now be following a track which runs between a hedge on your left and more fruit trees on the right. The track soon meets the crest of a ridge where there are good views ahead to the North Downs and the water tower on Gravelly Hill. It then proceeds downhill, passing the 14th tee on your right, to soon arrive at one of the greens. Pass to the left of the green, in the direction of a footpath sign and continue downhill following a hedge on your right. You should ignore a gap in the hedge as you progress and continue to pass to the right of another green, immediately after which the track forks. You should take the left hand fork, in the direction of another public footpath sign. The track now runs through a dense pine wood and also acts as a path between tees, so you may well find yourself in the thick of a number of golfers.

As the track reaches the other side of the pine wood, you should carry straight on, still following the footpath sign and head for a stile ahead, approximately fifty metres in the distance. Pass between two more tees to reach the stile which you should cross to continue along the right hand perimeter of a field. At the far side of the field on meeting a track, turn right to follow it along the left hand perimeter of another field, with the golf course now on your right. Take care here as the going can often be very muddy.

As you continue, the conveyor belt of some quarry works will come into view ahead and you will also see, where gaps in the hedge allow, another quarry to your left. This quarry is worked for Fuller's Earth, a product for which Godstone is famed, having been extracted here for centuries. The earth is a great absorber of grease and in the past was used to cleanse wool. It was once considered so valuable that during the reign of Edward II, its export was prohibited and a thriving smuggling industry sprang up. The track eventually ends at a tarmac lane beside two Victorian cottages on your left. Turn left along the lane which runs gently uphill and passes between the entrances to the quarry and the Quarry Garden. Stay on the lane, later passing a house on your left and after approximately one hundred and fifty metres, leave it to take a signposted footpath on the right, just before reaching "North Park Farm", visible ahead. To join the footpath you will have to cross a stile into a field. As you do so, immediately to your left are views beyond the M25 motorway to Gravelly Hill and to its right a wooded hill top which conceals Pilgrim hill fort.

Go diagonally right across the field, in the direction of a public footpath sign and at the far side go over a stile and continue ahead along a path which runs between an avenue of hawthornes as well as between two old quarry works. The latter, in part, now act as reservoirs for East Surrey Water. Pass through a kissing gate, thereby leaving the quarries behind, and carry straight on along a prominent path which runs across the centre of a small field, where the first houses of Godstone are now in view ahead.

On meeting the perimeter fencing at the left hand side of the field, pass through another kissing gate and turn right along a track (notice the sign here stating the Law & Property Act of 1925, protecting the greens in and around Godstone). The track soon passes between cottages to arrive in front of the village green and conveniently, almost next to "The Hare and Hounds", free house.

Godstone (OS. 350516 Map 187) *is a picture book village set around a large green with a pond at one corner. Unfortunately, the scene is spoilt somewhat by the busy A25 and the B2236 which, together, enclose two sides of the green. If you can ignore the traffic, exploring Godstone will bring its own rewards with the many different styles of houses each having their own stories to tell, some with topsyturvy extensions giving a romantic image to a working past. The setting of Godstone is relatively recent, the village growing out of the leather industry in the Elizabethan period. Later, the village became famous for its iron works and the manufacture of gunpowder, before the Evelyn's transferred its centre to Chilworth (see "Gunpowder Encounter" in "10 Adventurous Walks in Surrey").*

The name Godstone, like the village, is fairly recent. During Saxon times the area was known as Wachelestede, which translated, means "fulling place", referring to the Fullers earth found here. It is believed the current name is also derived from the ground, praising the quality of the soil on which the village stands, God's stone.

The most famous building in the village is "The White Hart", Beefeater. The building is Elizabethan, though it is known that an inn has stood on this site since the reign of Richard II. The road on which it stands is originally Roman, taking people from the south coast to London. For centuries, it was the main route to the sea and the inn became a stop-over for numerous famous people, including George IV and Queen Victoria. In the 18th century, Sir Robert Clayton of Bletchingley purchased the inn, along with much of the village and "The White Hart" promptly became "The Clayton

Arms". It was not until earlier this century that the original name was restored. Today, the inn is a Beefeater restaurant and the company, in fairness, has done its best to retain the inn's original character.

Apart from "The White Hart", Godstone has two more hostelries and an hotel. "The Hare and Hounds" dates from Tudor times and is a popular local, serving a wide range of beers as well as food. At the southern end of the green is "The Bell", Friary Meux. This is another pub with character dating from the 14th century and offers accommodation as well as food. The hotel is simply called "The Godstone Hotel" and has a popular and reasonably priced restaurant, "The Coach House".

At "The Hare and Hounds", turn left along a tarmac path which passes in front of the pub and continue to now follow the busy main road, the A25, until you reach a zebra crossing on your right. Go over the crossing over the A25 to reach a road island. Here you should carry straight on, crossing another road, the B2236, (ignoring a second zebra crossing on your right). At the other side, turn right along Godstone's main shopping street, in the direction of the sign for "Godstone Farm".

Pass "The White Hart", opposite the village pond and take a tarmac lane left which is signposted to the Parish church, immediately after. The lane immediately leads into a car park belonging to the White Hart Barn, the village hall. Pass to the right of the hall and follow a tarmac path, known locally as The Bay Path, ahead to shortly pass a beautiful pond on the left. This is Bay Pond, once a hammer pond serving the iron industry. The name Bay refers to the damm built to retain the water. Today, it belongs to the Surrey Wildlife Trust and is run as a nature reserve.

After the pond follow the path which rises gently to reach a part of Godstone that most visitors rarely see or visit, a hamlet dominated by and taking its name from a church, namely Church Town.

i **Church Town (OS. 357515 Map 187)** *is a quite unexpected and beautiful hamlet, occupying the site of an early Saxon settlement. You arrive at a lane in front of the church which sits on a large knoll, its spire stretching skywards. Either side of the lane sit a cluster of picture postcard cottages, which are worth more than a few minutes attention. To the right of the churchyard are Godstone's almshouses. Despite their appearance, they were built in the 19th century from designs by Sir Gilbert Scott, who was also responsible for the Albert Memorial and St. Pancras station in London. Scott lived at nearby "Rooksnest". The church, dedicated to St. Nicholas, sits on the foundations of a Norman church. The current building dates from the early 13th century and was heavily restored in 1872 by Sir Gilbert. The most interesting part of the church is the Evelyn Chapel which houses the tomb of Sir John Evelyn and his wife, Dame Tomasin. It is dated 1664. Several other memorial tablets remember the Evelyn family who dominated life in this village during the 16th and 17th centuries, before moving to Wotton. In the churchyard is the grave of Walker Miles who was the pioneer of rambling clubs. Walker incidentally, was his original name and not one he adopted.*

To continue our route, cross the lane and pass through the lychgate to join a path which runs through the churchyard, passing to the right of the church. After the church, the path runs downhill through the extensive but beautiful churchyard and at the far side, meets a tarmac crossing path. Ignore this to pass through a gap in a fence and continue ahead along a narrow path marked by a yellow arrow as a public footpath.

The footpath immediately bends right to reach and cross an ornate bridge, after which you will pass to the right of a small but beautiful pond complete with hungry ducks. Continue to cross a second bridge and follow the footpath as it bends right to run through a small copse, at the end of which it continues between a line of ornamental firs which act as a formal entrance to the grounds of a large house. The footpath then runs uphill across the centre of a small field and at the far side, progresses naturally into a more prominent path which soon bends right. You will now walk between banks and should follow the path as it bends left to arrive at another field.

On meeting the field, turn right in the direction of a footpath sign and follow the right hand field perimeter, now going downhill. Before reaching the end of the field, the path meets a track on the right and you should turn left onto it, now following a marked public bridleway. The bridleway soon bends left passing the magnificent "Leigh Place", (once home to the Evelyn family), after which you should look out for a marked public footpath on the right. Go over a stile to join the public footpath and follow it downhill between fences and gardens to pass between two ponds at the bottom.

i

After the ponds, turn left over a stile and follow another public footpath over a bridge and continue along the right hand bank of one of the ponds. At the other side of the pond, the path arrives at the entrance on your right to the beautiful "Leigh Mill House". *It is now hard to believe that this beautiful mill with its tranquil ponds was built by the Evelyn's in the 16th century for the sole purpose of manufacturing gunpowder. Manufacturing continued here until 1637 when it was transferred to Chilworth.* Turn right along a signposted public bridleway which takes you between a tennis court on your left and the mill house on your right.

i

After the tennis court you will arrive at a "T" junction where you should turn left along a signposted public footpath (part of the Greensand Way), initially bordered by some well kept hedges. This passes yet another pond on your right and a wooded knoll on your left. *The knoll is the site of another lost castle and the pond, along with the one beside "Leigh Mill House", are the remains of its moat. Little is known of its history except that it was probably Norman, built at roughly the same time as the castle at Bletchingley. Today, there are virtually no signs of its existence and you will have to stretch your imagination to picture the scene all those centuries ago. Incidentally, if an animal crosses your path at this point, be very wary as not far from here there once lived a witch. She was said to be able to turn herself into the form of an animal at will!*

i

A short distance later, pass through a kissing gate ignoring another footpath off to the left, to arrive at the main road, the A22. Cross the road, pass through a kissing gate the other side and continue ahead along the left hand perimeter of a field. After passing over a ridge you will see the first signs of the village of Tandridge, our next destination. Follow the field perimeter gently downhill where to your left, you will gain good views across to the North Downs. At the far side of the field the path becomes a track and continues through a strip of woodland. Thereafter, you should stay on the track as it crosses the centre of a field and then continues between the first houses of Tandridge to reach a road.

Tandridge (OS. 373507 Map 187) *is a small village set on the edge of the Greensand Ridge and despite its size, gives its name to the district council. The village church is at the northern end of the village on top of the ridge. It dates from*

i
✝

the 13th century but it is the churchyard yew which holds your attention. It has a girth of thirtytwo and a half feet, making it one of the largest in Surrey if not the country. Beneath its branches is the tomb of the architect, Sir Gilbert Scott.

Tandridge once had a priory run by a small settlement of Austin Canons (Augustinian monks). This disappeared at the time of the dissolution of the monasteries, though one of the gravestones in the churchyard is said to have come from the priory.

Just east of the church stands "Tandridge Court", a classical style house set in magnificent grounds. One of its more important owners was Bostock Fuller, a Justice of the Peace during the reign of Elizabeth I. The village is one of few in Surrey still to have a working blacksmith and it also has a large hostelry in the form of "The Barley Mow", a free house. The pub has a large restaurant on which it bases its reputation. It also serves some good beer.

To continue our route, cross the road and turn right to pass "The Barley Mow". Ignore a signposted public footpath on the left, thereby leaving the Greensand Way, and carry straight on along the road passing the village school on the right, beside which stands the covering for the old village well. After the school stay on the road, leaving the houses of Tandridge behind and continue until you see a signposted public footpath at the other side of the road, beside a speed limit sign. Cross the road to join the footpath, passing over a stile into a field.

Carry straight on along the left hand perimeter of the field, now going downhill and take time to enjoy good views ahead to Tilburstow Hill. On nearing the bottom of the valley as the field perimeter begins to turn right, take a narrow footpath left which continues downhill and meanders through a thicket. Take care not to miss it. The path soon takes you across a bridge over the beautiful Gibbs Brook, after which you should continue ahead across a narrow field and at the far side, cross a stile into another field. Continue ahead along the right hand field perimeter now going gently uphill, up the other side of the valley.

On reaching the corner of the field, go over a stepped stile and carry straight on across the next field in the direction of a yellow footpath arrow. If the way is unclear, then as a guide, the path is at first about twenty metres in from the left hand field perimeter and meets it at the far side (the opposite corner). At this point, go over a stile and bear diagonally right across a field, heading for a gap in the hedge ahead (if you find yourself crossing a stream, then you will not have gone far enough right to reach the hedge).

Pass through the gap in the hedge into another field and carry straight on following a line of oak trees. At the field end, go over a stile to arrive once again at the main road, the A22. Turn left along the A22 for approximately twenty metres to arrive at a bus stop. Cross the road here and join a signposted public footpath the other side, at first crossing a stile into a field to do so. Go diagonally right across the field heading for the field perimeter the other side, which is right of a house visible ahead. You should reach the field perimeter just as it bends right and here, should cross a stile on your right into another field. (If you find yourself passing the house mentioned or following the field perimeter round to the right, then you will have gone too far and should retrace your steps).

Once in the field, go diagonally right heading for a spot roughly in the centre at the far side. As you cross there are views left to the imposing "Orme House" and to your right, to the North Downs. As you progress, Tandridge will also come into view. At the far side of the field, go over a stile and continue across the next field in the same direction to meet and cross another stile beside a metal gate at the field end. (If you find yourself at a pair of metal gates, do not pass through them as you are too far left and should therefore, go right along the perimeter). After going over the stile you will meet a track, again part of the Greensand Way, onto which you should turn left to follow it along the side of Brakey Hill. The track affords excellent views south across the Weald to the South Downs. The large house you can see (a little further on), has recently been converted into luxury apartments, a modern trend which preserves many old buildings that would otherwise fall into disrepair.

The track eventually arrives at a road, the original Roman road which passes through Godstone, beside a huge beech tree the roots of which have grown so high as to almost form a small cave **(OS. 354499)**. Cross the road and join a sandy track the other side, marked as a public bridleway as well as the Greensand Way. The track follows the edge of Tilburstow Hill and shortly bends right to pass through a large bank, after which it divides to enter two fields. You should go into the right hand field and immediately upon entering, turn left to follow a fence on your left and a line of newly planted fir trees on the right.

After a short distance, the track follows the perimeter of the wood which covers the top of Tilburstow Hill, with views opening out to the south as you progress. Ignore a marked footpath off to the right and when the wood bends right to occupy the higher slopes of the hill, stay on the track which carries straight on between fields and at the other side, forks. You should take the left hand fork and continue ahead to soon reach a stile beside a metal gate. Go over the stile and continue along the right hand perimeter of a field, where there are yet more good views south.

Just before you reach the far side of the field where you will see a beautiful half timbered cottage on the left, leave the field perimeter by taking a narrow path right. Take great care not to miss this. The path leads to a stile which you should cross to arrive at a lane. Turn left along the lane and sometime on, ignore a signposted footpath off to the right. Continue until you see a signposted public bridleway on the right, also marked by the familiar blue "GW" of the Greensand Way. Take this to join a track which passes in front of the cottage mentioned earlier and then proceeds along the left hand perimeter of a field passing a pond on your left.

The track twists with the field perimeter and passes another pretty cottage on your right, complete with a conservatory that takes full advantage of the enviable views. After the cottage, the track passes another house before arriving at a "T" junction in the form of a narrow tarmac lane. Turn left along the lane, thereby maintaining the same direction and pass to the right of a large house. The lane then bends left and you should leave it here and join a path ahead, signposted as a public bridleway. The bridleway runs along the side of another hill, Gravel Hill, which forms part of the Greensand Ridge, the name of the hill giving an instant clue as to the nature of the quarrying carried out here. The quarry is hidden behind a hedged bank on your right.

Stay on the bridleway which can be very muddy, even in dry weather and ignore all turnings off to later meet a fork. Take the left hand fork and maintain your route, as before still ignoring any turnings off, and follow it as it later bends right to arrive at a concrete drive, the entrance to the quarry just passed. Cross the drive and go up a bank heading slightly to the right, to join a fairly prominent path leading across a grass area which is reclaimed land from the quarry. The path at first, can be a little undefined but

I have been informed that this will soon be signposted to avoid confusion.

At the other side, pass through a gap in the hedge to reach a semi-tarmacced path onto which you should turn left. Keep to the semi-tarmacced path, ignoring all turnings off, to shortly pass a murky pond on the left. There are good views at this point on your right to Bletchingly, a good indication that we are nearing the end of the walk. After the pond the path arrives at a tarmac drive onto which you should turn right to meet a road. Turn right along the road to pass between the first houses of Bletchingly and after approximately one hundred metres, take a signposted public footpath left. This takes you up steps and then follows the perimeter fencing of some gardens on your right before continuing between fields. The footpath eventually arrives at another road, Castle Square.

i **Bletchingley Castle (OS. 322506 Map 187).** *Directly in front of you at the other side of the road, stands a house and behind it in part of its grounds, an area of scrub and small copse. This is the site of the once powerful castle of Bletchingley and a footpath signposted to Nutfield leads around what was once the base of the castle's ramparts with rewarding views that were so valuable to the castle's defenders.*

The castle, it is believed, was built by the powerful Richard de Tonbridge, head of the de Clare family, after the Norman conquest. At this time and into the next century, castle building was rampant as the barons sought to secure their futures. Four at least, are known to have been built in Surrey alone.

The de Clare's continued to play a major role in the running of the country. This often brought them into conflict with the King which ultimately brought the destruction of the castle. The first major conflict came in 1170, when the residing Earl of Clare despatched a garrison from Bletchingley castle to Canterbury to protect Thomas a Beckett, who it was strongly rumoured, Henry II was about to have killed. The rest is history, the garrison failed and the Archbishop was murdered at the alter of his cathedral (see "In Pilgrims' Footsteps").

In the next century, came an even greater conflict and one that had a personal note. The sixth Earl of Clare, Richard, married a lady called Amicia, whose sister was wife to the infamous King John. The King later literally dumped Amicia's sister for his mistress, Isabella d'Angouleme, and added insult to injury by refusing to return the wealth and land he had inherited through his marriage. Consequently and foolishly, he became an immediate enemy of the de Clare's. Richard got his revenge when he played a major part in the barons' revolt against the King, which culminated in the signing of the Magna Carta. At the head of the list of guarantors for the Magna Carta is Richard's name, along with that of his son, Gilbert, a measure of his contempt and mistrust of King John.

The de Clare's lack of trust for the King continued through to another generation and Gilbert's son, better known as the Red Earl, strongly supported the then leader of the barons, Simon de Montfort, Earl of Leicester. In 1258, the barons lead by de Montfort forced Henry III to sign the Reforming Provisions of Oxford, which effectively created our first Parliament. Instead of helping to ease matters, the treaty only helped to increase the conflict between the barons and the King. De Montfort filled the Parliament, which consisted of just twentyfive seats, with his supporters and as a result the Parliament became his mouth piece which the King simply ignored. The result was armed conflict and the consequential distruction of Bletchingley castle which was seen as a barons stronghold. The Red Earl was away at the time, fighting on the side of de Montfort at the Battle of Lewes. The battle was a victory for the barons at which Henry III was captured. In retaliation a Royal garrison recognising the castle's vulnerability with many of its defenders fighting at Lewes, attacked Bletchingley razing the castle to the ground and destroying much of the village in merciless revenge. In the following year, de Montfort was defeated and horribly killed at the Battle of Evesham. The Red Earl, perhaps recognising the way the scales were tipping, fought for the King at this battle, earning himself the reputation of traitor, a title which is only now being questioned.

Ironically, the Red Earl's son's loyalty to the King (then Edward II), brought an abrupt end to the de Clare line when he was killed at the disastrous Battle of Bannockburn in 1314. The barons went on without the de Clare's to again oppose the King, led by a new duo, Sir Philip de la Beche (featured in "10 Adventurous Walks in Berkshire") and Thomas, Earl of Lancaster, which resulted in civil war in 1321.

Standing in the smart suburban side streets of this pretty village, it is hard to imagine the castle and the colourful people it protected. Harder still to imagine, is the bloody one-sided battle which raged here in 1264 and the horrible death and suffering that resulted. Today, with little evidence on the ground that it ever existed, the castle could almost be forgotten and probably would be, if it were not for such a frequent use of the word "castle" in street and house names. Scant recognition for a building whose owners not only built Bletchingley, but helped lay the foundations on which our freedom is based today.

Turn right along the road to shortly reach the A25, the main High Street at Bletchingly. Cross the A25 and turn right along the pavement passing the attractive period houses of Bletchingly, to soon arrive at the war memorial, our starting point. Watching the cars speed along the village High Street, you cannot help wondering how many of their occupants see beyond the pretty tiled facias of the houses and if they know of the role a Bletchingley family played in their freedom today. The answer is sadly, very few but perhaps if you take time to enjoy a well deserved drink at one of the many watering holes in the village, you can pass on your discovery of a lost castle in the hope that their next visit will not be a flying one!

ACCOMMODATION

The Godstone Hotel, Godstone. Tel: 0883 742461
On the walk, this is a picturesque 16th century hotel with a popular restaurant. It has the added attraction of being set in Godstone, one of Surrey's more beautiful villages.

The Whyte Harte, Bletchingley. Tel: 0883 843231
On the walk, this inn which dates originally from 1388, despite some modernisation, has largely maintained many old features allowing you in part, to relive history.

Youth Hostel, Tanners Hatch YHA, Polesden Lacey, Dorking.
Tel: 0372 52528
Approximately twelve miles from the walk, Tanners Hatch is an isolated cottage (you can only reach it by foot). Situated in the woods of Ranmore Common, the hostel has no electricity so bring your own lighting. Camping is also permitted.

Camping and Caravanning, Rose Dene Farm, Godstone. Tel: 0342 892586
Approximately one mile from the walk, this is a lovely secluded site with the advantage of being well run and having its own farm shop.

THE BOX HILL BONE BREAKER

Distance: 9½ miles (15.25 km)
Time: Allow approximately 5 hours
Map: Ordnance Survey Landranger Map 187

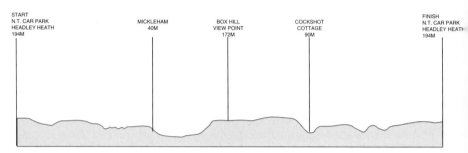

START
N.T. CAR PARK
HEADLEY HEATH
194M

MICKLEHAM
40M

BOX HILL
VIEW POINT
172M

COCKSHOT
COTTAGE
90M

FINISH
N.T. CAR PARK
HEADLEY HEATH
194M

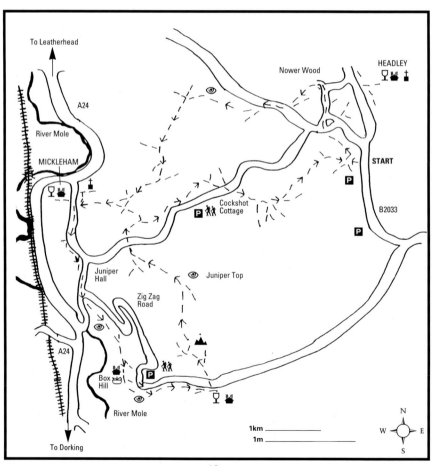

To Leatherhead

Nower Wood

HEADLEY

A24

River Mole

MICKLEHAM

START

P

Cockshot
Cottage

P

B2033

P

Juniper
Hall

Juniper Top

Zig Zag
Road

A24

Box
Hill

P

River Mole

1km
1m

N
W   E
S

12

Walk Summary

The Box Hill Bone Breaker is the sister walk to the Box Hill Bone Shaker ("10 Adventurous Walks in Surrey"), which I hope you survived! This time, the walk explores the countryside to the north and east of Box Hill. Starting at Headley, the walk follows some ancient tracks across Headley Heath and Mickleham Downs before climbing the famous Burford Spur of Box Hill to reach the summit. The return journey involves taking some spectacular and lesser known routes over Juniper Top and along the side of White Hill back to Headley. The countryside is beautiful at all times and there is much to keep you interested along the way, including frequent magnificent views. This does not come without some effort and there are several steep climbs and descents. Ensure you are fairly fit before attempting this walk.

Start - OS. 205539 Map 187

The walk starts from the National Trust car park off the B2033 at Headley Heath. There are several car parks on this road but this one is easily identified as it is opposite a cricket pitch just south of Headley itself. By car, getting there is fairly straight forward. From the south and west, the B2033 is reached by taking the B2032 between the A217 and the A25. From the north and east, the B2033 is best joined at its junction with the A24 (a roundabout), just outside Leatherhead.

The nearest railway station is at West Humble and from there it is under a mile walk to join the walk at the bottom of Burford Spur (OS. 171523). An alternative start can be made from Cockshott Wood car park below White Hill (OS. 189536) or the car park at the top of Box Hill (OS. 179512). Both the car parks at Headley and Box Hill belong to the National Trust which have made them "Pay and Display", although if you are a member and display your card, parking is free.

THE BOX HILL BONE BREAKER

From the car park walk with your back to the road and leave the car park, passing through a gap in the bank. Thereafter, walk straight ahead across an open grass play area, at the far side of which you will meet a crossing track. Turn right along the track and continue for approximately two hundred and fifty metres, ignoring all minor turnings off, until you see a turning right marked by a wooden tree stump and a blue arrow. As a guide, there is a silver birch in the middle of the track here and to your right, a red brick house.

Take the turning right in the direction of the house mentioned and go downhill for a few paces to then join a narrow lane on your left. Follow the lane ahead, maintaining your route straight on, now going uphill. Just as you meet a perimeter hedge of holly bushes to the left of the lane, turn left onto a narrow crossing path. This immediately runs parallel with the holly hedge on your right and you should continue to follow the path, going gently downhill, to later arrive at a track, signposted as Crabtree Lane. Turn right along the track to meet and cross a road, the B2033, and join a tarmac lane the other side, signposted as Tumber Street.

Follow Tumber Street through the outskirts of Headley village passing between some beautiful cottages and ignore all turnings off until the lane bends sharp right. Here you should leave it to take a signposted bridleway left, also signposted as Langley Lane. If you require some early refreshment however, or wish to visit Headley village centre which is no more than a quarter of a mile detour, continue along the lane until you arrive at a "T" junction and there, turn right to arrive at

"The Cock Inn", Friary Meux. You will have to retrace your steps to rejoin our route at Langley Lane.

The village of Headley (OS. 205548 Map 187) *is what my grandmother would call a "town village". In the countryside it remains under constant threat from the burgeoning London suburbs and the M25. A village it still is but the absence of any real farming and a number of relatively modern houses, along with the over-modernisation of the 18th century "Cock Inn", gives it a suburban feel, a "town village".*

The Faithful Family Vault

The church, which is situated behind "The Cock Inn", is Victorian and was completed in 1859. As you enter the churchyard you are greeted by some of the remains of the original church which has been made into what looks like a minature grotto. This is in fact, the Faithful family vault and typical of Victorian fantasy architecture. The position of the original church, which was probably Saxon, is marked by a number of clipped box trees which give nearby Box Hill its name. A sundial with an inscription in latin, "I am nothing without light from above", is set into the south porch. Inside there is little of great interest, although the wood panelling of the nave is said to have come from Newgate prison when it was demolished to make way for the Old Bailey. Just outside the churchyard the Surrey office of the Association of Boys Clubs occupies what was once the village school.

"The Cock Inn", once a small village pub, now has a modern extension and a large car park to cater for trade from the nearby London suburbs. The original bar is basic and has a good atmosphere. The lounge which includes a restaurant, is situated in the extension and is quite plush, decorated with a rustic flavour. Outside, a sign welcomes walkers which is reassuring, especially if you have specifically made a detour for a drink!

Returning to our route, once on Langley Lane ignore a stile on the left and continue along the track passing first a cottage and then a house on your left. After the house, the track runs gently uphill between banks along the perimeter of Nower Wood which belongs to the Surrey Wildlife Trust and is run as a nature reserve. Stay on the track ignoring all turnings off to eventually arrive at a road, the B2033, where there are views ahead across to Ashurst Rough, Lodge Hill and the Box Hill Gap.

Turn right along the road taking care of the traffic and after approximately fifty metres, you will meet a parking area on your left. Two bridleways fork out of the parking area and you should take the right hand bridleway, which initially runs through scrub and then along the perimeter of Tyrrells Wood golf course on your right. Stay on the bridleway ignoring all turnings off, for approximately three quarters of a mile until you meet a wide track ahead and a metal gate on your left. As a guide before reaching this point, you will pass a beautiful line of beech trees and also, when the bridleway breaks from the wood, you will enjoy excellent views ahead to your left to Ranmore Common and on a clear day, the prominent spire of Ranmore church.

On meeting the wide track in front of you, join this to continue ahead and ignore a track leading off to the right. After approximately twenty paces, turn left onto another track marked by a red arrow. This is the Roman Stane Street, known locally as Pebble Lane. The track leads downhill for a short distance, going over a crossing track and passes a large property, "The Garden House", on the right. Continue downhill to the bottom of a valley where you should ignore another crossing track and go up the other side.

The track passes through scrubland, which in summer includes the flowering buddleia or butterfly bush, easily recognised by its distinct mauve funnel shaped flowers and the mass of butterflies surrounding them. Incidentally, this area of scrubland was once proud woodland but was sadly devastated by the infamous storm of 1987. Stay on the track to eventually meet a fork in front of a National Trust sign for Mickleham Downs. Carry straight on here, taking the left hand fork, to go up a bank and follow the track as it bends right and then left to climb gently uphill through woodland.

Buddleia - The Butterfly Bush

The track soon levels out and runs in a straight line through the wood. To avoid the sometimes muddy horse tracks here, there is a small path that you can take which runs parallel to the track on the left. Sometime on, you will meet a crossing track marked by a wooden post and blue arrow. Turn right here and continue to later arrive at another crossing track. This time, turn left in the direction of a red arrow and after a few paces, ignore a path off to the right and continue straight on. Ignore two further paths off to the left and right respectively beside a National Trust sign and map.

Shortly after the National Trust sign the track begins to descend and you should ignore another track off to the left blocked, at the time of writing, by a metal bar. Follow the track, passing through more buddleia bushes and where gaps allow, take time to enjoy the views to your right across the Mole Gap. Soon after passing another National Trust sign, this time for Mickleham Downs, turn right between two posts to join a narrow crossing path, a footpath marked by a yellow arrow **(OS. 177535)**.

The footpath runs steeply downhill through undergrowth which can be quite dense in summer. In wet weather, it can also be extremely slippery and great care is needed to avoid too speedy a descent! As you near the bottom the footpath follows the line of some fields on your left, where there are lovely views across the fields to Ranmore Common, the other side of the Mole Gap.

You will eventually meet a stile beside a white gate which you should cross to join a track. Continue ahead along the track which takes you to the village of Mickleham and leads out beside the village church.

i

Mickleham (OS. 171535 Map 187) *is a village of smart well kept houses nestling at the bottom of Mickleham Downs. It is perfectly described by the 19th century writer, John Timbs, as "a genteel village". The church though restored, maintains its Norman tower and it was here that two famous novelists were married, George Meredith and Fanny Burney. Fanny Burney also met her husband, General d'Arblay, at Mickleham. Before leaving, note the wooden graves in the churchyard which are probably the best preserved in Surrey.*

The village hostelry is "The Running Horses", a free house and a fine 17th century pub. The pub sign commemorates the winning of the Derby by Gadland in 1828 after a dead heat. The sign depicts the dead heat on one side and the winner on the other. This interpretation of the pub name is fairly recent, the sign used to depict another winner of the Derby, Blair Athol, who was first past the post in 1864 and was stabled in the village. The pub itself can genuinely be called a local pub and apart from serving some good beer, offers the customer some wholesome food in the form of bar meals as well as The Stable restaurant. The bar is unspoilt by modern interior designers and retains an atmosphere created by hundreds of satisfied customers over the centuries. A visit to the toilets is a must as they still have many of the original brass fittings.

To continue from where the track arrives at Mickleham beside the church, cross the road and turn left along the pavement the other side. Follow the road for approximately a quarter of a mile, ignoring a public footpath off to your right at the end of a brick and flint wall, and shortly after, join a second signposted public footpath on the right which runs parallel to the road and follow it to its end. On your way you will pass the magnificent "Juniper Hall" on your left.

i

Juniper Hall (OS. 172525 Map 187) *is a spellbinding 18th century house in a superb location at the opening of a valley which divides White and Lodge Hill. In its grounds, several grand cedar trees enhance the picture.*

In 1792, the hall was rented to several French aristocrats who acquired the building as a refuge from the excesses of the French Revolution. Among the refugees were some notable names including Talleyrand and Madame Stael. General d'Arblay was another and it was at the hall that he met his future bride, Fanny Burney. Fanny, who nicknamed the hall "Juniper Hole" because of its location, allowed d'Arblay to become her French tutor and within a year the two were married.

Juniper Hall is now owned by the National Trust who run it as a field studies centre.

The footpath ends by going down some steps to meet a public footpath sign at the road. Do not cross the road in the direction of the footpath sign, but continue straight on instead along the pavement. Look out for the start of a pavement at the other side of the road soon after, where you should cross the road to join it and continue ahead. On meeting a road on your left signposted to Box Hill, cross this and at the other side ignore a bridleway which leads left uphill and also a signposted public footpath which follows the road ahead. You should take a grass path instead between the bridleway and footpath, which runs gently uphill. This leads to the famous grass buttress on the western side of Box Hill, Burford Spur, and if you have overindulged at "The Running Horses" you may be about to regret it!

Follow the path up the distinct grass slope of Box Hill, the open grass hillside here offering an open invitation for rests along the way and views across the Mole Gap to Ranmore Common and "Norbury Park". On a clear day, you may also see Leith Hill and Dorking and in the valley below, the newly created Denbies Vineyard. If you have walked "The Box Hill Bone Shaker" in "10 Adventurous Walks in Surrey", then you will also recognise much of the route from here.

At the top of the hill, follow a prominent chalk path ahead where you will very probably meet hoards of people who have got to the top of the hill the easy way, by car! This is a well worn path and follows the top of the famous Box Hill cliff. Sometime later, the path forks and you should take the right hand fork to carry straight on along the top of the cliff. After a short distance you will pass the gravestone of Major Labelliere.

The grave of Major Peter Labelliere (OS. 176516 Map 187) *is also a monument* *i* *to the English eccentric. Labelliere was a well known local eccentric who left instructions that upon his death he was to be buried upside down on Box Hill, where he used to enjoy roaming on a stormy day. His reason for this peculiar request was so that on Judgement Day when the whole world is turned upside down, he would be turned right way up to meet his Maker. Not only was he buried upside down, he was also buried some way underground, one hundred feet to be exact. It is said that his ghost now walks the hill and if you are ever on the hill when the wind and rain are at their strongest and the day trippers are safe at home in front of their television sets, then it is very easy to imagine this larger than life character roaming the hillside.*

After the gravestone, the path forks again and this time you should take the left hand fork to continue along the top of the hill, enjoying excellent views right to Dorking. The path leads out to a junction of tracks. On your right here are the gates *i* to "Swiss Cottage", where John Logie Baird (1888-1946), the inventor of television pictures, once lived and experimented. From here, take a path which runs between a track on your left and another which leads straight ahead. This leads to another path onto which you should turn left to reach the National Trust Visitors Centre which has a shop and Information Room. There is also a National Trust cafe here.

From the Visitors Centre, start to retrace your steps but do not rejoin the path on which you arrived on your right. Instead continue ahead along a path which runs parallel to the road on your left, called the Zig Zag road because of its route up the hill. This leads to a direction finder on the southern side of Box Hill with yet more ◉ good views, this time south across the Weald to the South Downs. *The stone* *i* *direction finder (171m / 561ft), is dedicated to Leopald Salomans of nearby "Norbury Park", who in 1914 gave Box Hill "to the nation". Unfortunately, apart from the cafe, this is usually the most popular spot on Box Hill with hoards of people all seemingly trying to get as close to their neighbour as possible. I advise a quick escape!*

Viewpoint at
Box Hill

Pass the direction finder to join part of the route in "The Box Hill Boneshaker", also part of the North Downs Way marked by the distinctive white acorns. Immediately after the path leaves the grass slope, leave the main path and take a path left still marked as the North Downs Way. Take care not to miss it. This leads gently uphill to almost meet the road and continues, running parallel to the road, to later arrive at semi-open grass hillside once more and a wooden seat, a convenient place for a rest and away from the crowds.

After the wooden seat, the path continues through woodland, still part of the North Downs Way and therefore, marked by the white acorns. It then later continues to cross a ditch by way of some wooden steps and almost immediately after, meets a second set of steps, this time crossing a wide track. Do not cross the track but turn left instead to follow it, thereby leaving the North Downs Way, to shortly arrive at a car park to "La Collina", a restaurant and free house though not really suitable for walkers.

Turn left through the car park to reach and cross the road which runs along the top of Box Hill and join a public bridleway the other side. This takes the form of a prominent path which runs through woodland across the top of the hill. Sometime later, ignore a marked track off to the right and stay on the bridleway, ignoring further turnings off to the left and right, to eventually reach a crossing track.

Turn right along the crossing track and continue for a few paces where you will meet another track joining from the left, marked by a National Trust horse track sign. You should ignore this to carry straight on. Further on, the track forks and you should take the left hand fork to now go gently downhill, ignoring any turnings off. Your route will take you through more beautiful woodland along the edge of Ashurst Rough. Where gaps in the trees allow, you will also gain glorious views to your left across to Fetcham Downs.

Eventually, you will reach a kissing gate through which you should pass to leave the wood and arrive at the open hillside of Juniper Top (165m/541ft). Continue ahead along a prominent grass path to shortly arrive at a wide expanse of shorter grass, the work of rabbits, at the very edge of the hill. *From here you can enjoy yet more stunning views across the Mole Gap to "Norbury Park", Fetcham Downs and Ranmore Common. Directly below you is the grand building passed at the beginning of the walk, "Juniper Hall". Unlike Box Hill, Juniper Top cannot be reached by car and unless you know it, is fairly difficult to find. Consequently, meeting another person here is a rarity and perhaps selfishly, you can enjoy one of the most beautiful spots in Surrey with only nature for company.*

To continue, go straight down the centre of the grass spur leading from Juniper Top, taking care not to end up rolling down the hill as you admire the views ahead! Half way down the hill you will pass a bench where you can rest, though I rather think this was errected for people climbing the hill as opposed to those descending. The descent however, is long and quite difficult and you will now understand why I decided to call this walk "The Box Hill Bone Breaker"!

As you near the bottom of the hill, you will pass through a lovely silver birch wood. At the very bottom, pass through a kissing gate beside a larger metal gate and turn right thereafter, along a track to shortly arrive at a small parking area **(OS. 177529)**. Walk through the parking area, cross a lane ahead and join a signposted footpath the other side, which leads up the side of Juniper Hill. The reason for such a frequency in the name Juniper is the juniper bush which grows in profusion

18

around these hills.

The Juniper *is an evergreen that produces a fruit in the form of a dark blue berry* *which takes two years to ripen. Juniper berries are mainly used to flavour drink, most commonly gin. In France they are used to make another alcoholic beverage, genevrette, and in Sweden a form of beer, though I'm not sure I would recommend it! If you are teetotal then all is not lost, as this versatile fruit can also be roasted, ground and mixed with boiling water to make a reasonable drink with a taste similar to that of coffee.*

The way up Juniper Hill is aided by steps albeit it is still a fairly hard climb and at this point, the only bones you currently feel like breaking are probably mine!

Further up the hill, the steps end but you however, must continue. Soon after, the path bends right and thankfully, at the same time, levels out to run along the side of the hill. The views to your right here are across to Juniper Top and Lodge Hill. Sometime on, look out for a narrow footpath leading off to the right opposite a bench, which you should take thereby leaving the main route. First though, I suggest you take a breather and rest on the bench where you will gain some different views back over the Mole Gap to Ranmore Common.

The footpath you have joined runs through woodland along the southern slope of White Hill. The sloping hillside here is extremely steep and great care is needed to avoid a fall. The path itself passes through a mixture of scrub and yews and in places can be a little overgrown in summer. At the time of writing at one point in particular, a fallen tree must be negotiated to continue your route. You are rewarded however, with a spectacular route which in places affords excellent views of the surrounding countryside and sometime later, over "Warren Farm" which nestles in the valley below.

On nearing the valley bottom, the path passes through a yew wood and then more scrub to meet another path (as a guide, the total distance from joining this path opposite the bench to this point is approximately three quarters of a mile). Turn right along the path you have just met, which shortly follows a line of horse chestnuts. Sometime later, pass between two wooden posts and continue ahead walking above a small parking area, Cockshott Wood car park, to soon meet a lane opposite "Cockshott Cottage", also beside a public bridleway sign **(OS. 189536 Map 187).**

Cross the lane and join a signposted public bridleway the other side, also marked as a National Trust Long Walk, and pass to the left of "Cockshott Cottage". Follow the bridleway as it climbs uphill between fields, near the top bending left through woodland and shortly after, right following an old flint wall on your right. Soon after, you will meet a track which leads downhill on your left, opposite a National Trust sign for Headley Heath. Take this, descending steeply, to reach a wide track at the bottom of the valley onto which you should turn left.

The track soon bends right to meet another track (a marked bridleway) on your right and a path on the left, marked as part of a National Trust Long Walk with a National Trust blue arrow. Take the latter to go fairly steeply uphill by way of some more bone breaking steps. These take you to the top of the hill where there is a welcoming bench and a National Trust path marker, the bench offering probably your last chance for a short break and perhaps a late picnic.

At the hill top, turn right in the direction of the blue National Trust arrow and continue, ignoring all turnings off, until the path forks beside another blue National Trust arrow. At this point, carry straight on (left hand fork), thereby leaving the National Trust Long Walk, to shortly meet a wide crossing track where a number of paths and tracks lead off in various directions. You should take the second track from the left, marked by a blue bridleway arrow, to maintain your route ahead.

Follow the track, ignoring any minor turnings off and at every fork, take the more prominent fork to eventually reach a wide crossing track, marked by a post with several blue arrows. As a guide, to your left, the first houses of Headley are in view. Turn right onto the crossing track (if you find yourself descending to reach a tarmac lane beside a house, then you will have gone too far and should retrace your steps). Continue for a short distance until you meet another crossing track, onto which you should turn left and cross the grass play area traversed at the start of our walk, to return to the car park and our starting point.

ACCOMMODATION

The Burford Bridge Hotel (THF), West Humble. Tel: 0306 884561
Half a mile from the walk. On the banks of the river Mole at the foot of Box Hill, the Burford Bridge Hotel is set in a natural beauty spot complimented by the hotel's well cared for grounds. The hotel is full of history, Nelson spent his last night here before leaving for the Battle of Trafalgar. The hotel has good restaurants and an outdoor heated swimming pool.

The Running Horses, Mickleham. Tel: 0372 372590
On the walk, the Running Horses is a very local pub serving good bar food and beer. It also has an excellent restaurant and offers bed and breakfast accommodation. The pub is in a good location opposite the village church. An excellent choice at the end of a hard day's walking.

Youth Hostel, Tanners Hatch YHA, Polesden Lacey, Dorking. Tel: 0372 52528
Approximately two and a half miles from the walk, Tanners Hatch is an isolated cottage (it can only be reached by foot). Situated in the woods of Ranmore Common, the hostel has no electricity so bring your own lighting. Camping is also permitted.

Camping, Polesden Lacey, Dorking. Tel: 0372 456844
Approximately three miles from the walk, this is a Camping and Caravanning Club site in a beautiful setting on an old cricket pitch in the grounds of Polesden Lacey House, N.T. Please note, only tents and trailers are permitted.

A DATE WITH THE DEVIL

Distance: 9¾ miles (15.5 km)
Time: Allow approximately 5 hours
Map: Ordnance Survey Landranger Map 186

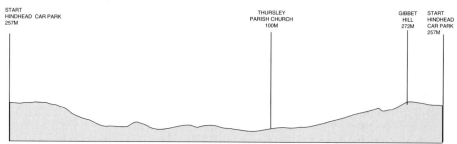

START
HINDHEAD CAR PARK
257M

THURSLEY
PARISH CHURCH
100M

GIBBET
HILL
272M

START
HINDHEAD
CAR PARK
257M

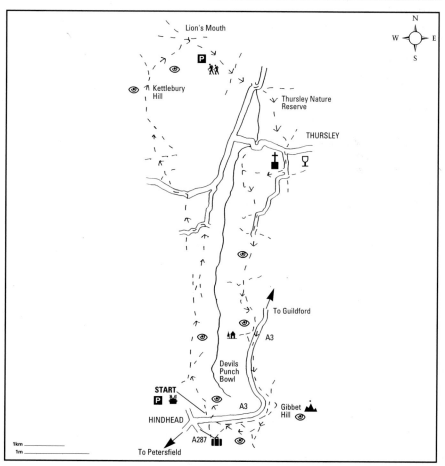

21

Walk Summary

A Date with the Devil explores the wild countryside around the Devil's Punch Bowl. For almost the whole route you are at one with nature with, at times, all signs of the 20th century out of sight. After skirting the western rim of the Devil's Punch Bowl, the route traverses the pine and heather clad army land of Hankley Common before returning via the beautiful village of Thursley. The last stretch follows the Greensand Way along the eastern rim of the Punch Bowl with the reward of probably some of the best view points in Surrey, including the famous Gibbet Hill. The going is fairly easy though one word of warning, it is easy when reaching the eastern rim of the Punch Bowl to relax and think you are almost home. Do not get caught out, it is still more than two miles to the finish. Relax too much and you may end up victim to the Devil!

Start - OS. 891358 Map 186

The walk starts from the Punch Bowl car park at Hindhead which doubles as a car park for the Hillcrest Cafe. The car park is marked by a blue "P" on the ordnance survey map. Getting there by car is easy as it is situated off the A3, almost opposite The Devil's Punch Bowl Hotel and just north of the traffic lights which control the junction of the A3 and the A287. If coming by train the nearest station is at Haslemere. From there it is possible to get a bus to Hindhead or, if you prefer, you can add an extra couple of miles to the walk by following the Greensand Way (marked on the map), to the start.

An alternative start can be made from the MOD controlled car park on Hankley Common (OS. 891411), though unless you are local this may be hard to find.

A DATE WITH THE DEVIL

The car park at Hindhead, especially on week days, is usually crowded with day trippers and lorry drivers who use the Hillcrest Cafe as a convenient half way stop over between London and Portsmouth. Crowds and lorries not being the ideal ingredient for a satisfying adventure, I suggest that you make hastily for the relative peace of the Devil's Punch Bowl. To do this, take a track to the right of the cafe, passing to the left of an information sign for Hindhead Common. The track is part of an overflow car park (lined by wooden stumps), where you should continue straight ahead passing between some of the wooden stumps and thereafter, passing to the right of a picnic bench and to the left of a Punch Bowl Nature Trail sign.

Continue ahead and go down some wide steps to arrive at a view point over the Devil's Punch Bowl. The view is breathtaking and you can immediately understand why this place is popular. Being only a few metres from the car park, unfortunately, the view point too is often crowded and therefore, I fear it is better that we learn of the history of this unique landscape at a quieter location. You will then better appreciate its dramatic beauty which has stirred such strong feelings in writers in the past.

To continue, from the view point take the first path left to pass a wooden pole marked by a blue arrow and to also pass behind a seat. You should ignore a tree stump which marks the start of a nature trail. As a guide, just after the seat you will pass another seat on your left and should now be walking along the western rim of the Punch Bowl, through beautiful woodland predominantly made up of ash and oak and interspersed with a small number of pines. The woodland floor is a carpet of bracken and hurtleberries.

Stay on the path ignoring all minor turnings off, to later meet and follow some fencing on your left. The path now follows the perimeter of the Punch Bowl and in places where gaps in the trees on your right allow, there are excellent views across the Punch Bowl to the North Downs beyond. Stay on the path to eventually meet a crossing track beside a National Trust sign for Highcomb **(OS. 887365)**, onto which you should turn right. Immediately after, ignore another track which forks right descending to the centre of the Punch Bowl.

The track you have joined continues to follow the rim of the Punch Bowl and again, in places you will be afforded beautiful views across the Punch Bowl to your right. Sometime on, the track passes beneath some telegraph wires after which it also forks. You should take the right hand fork, the more prominent track, and immediately after, take a path leading off to the right thereby leaving the main track. Take care not to miss it. The path is narrower and runs through the wood to shortly arrive at a seat, another excellent view point and the perfect place to learn of some of the history of the Devil's Punch Bowl.

The Devil's Punch Bowl. *A little way behind the seat is a stone memorial which* *i* *commemorates the gift of Highcomb Copse (which covers much of the Punch Bowl), to the National Trust by W.A. Robertson in memory of his brothers, both soldiers who were killed during the first World War. The Trust now owns approximately one thousand acres of land around Hindhead, much of it donated by local landowners like Mr. Robertson, encouraged by a visionary local councillor, Sir Robert Hunter, during the early part of this century. As you take in the breathtaking beauty of your surroundings, you will quickly realise the debt owed as a result of these generous donations, which virtually halted the rapid growth of Hindhead, a village in danger of destroying its popularity by developing the very resource that brought it fame. We will learn more of this later.*

Incredibly, before the coming of the railway at nearby Haslemere and the development of Hindhead, the heathland and the Punch Bowl was not looked upon as a place of beauty, but a landscape of desolation, superstition and fear. Few people lived in the area which was notorious for smugglers, highwaymen and other trades of dubious repute. Wells for drawing water hereabouts were bell-shaped, designed to conceal contraband. Superstitions also told of the bottom of the Punch Bowl being a place where no flora or vegetation survived and where no sane man would tread (a convenient story for the smugglers don't you think?).

Famous writers over the centuries confirmed the view of the common man, that the Punch Bowl and Hindhead was a place to be avoided. Jack Wilkes described the area as "dreary", Cobbett, who appeared to be particularly prejudiced, spoke of Hindhead and the Punch Bowl as being "certainly the most villainous spot that God ever made" and called Gibbet Hill (the other side of the Punch Bowl and on our route), a "miserable hill". J.E. Morris described the bottom of the Punch Bowl as a place of "desolate sterility", Samuel Pepys feared to pass this way at night and even Gilbert White of Selborne who took such an interest in his natural surroundings, did not write fondly of the area.

The natural death of a sailor and the brutal murder of another in the 18th century, only added to the Punch Bowl's reputation as a dark and dangerous place. Charles Dickens captured the cumulative thoughts of his fellow writers by including the story of the murdered sailor in his tale, "Nicholas Nickleby". Sitting at the edge of the Punch Bowl, Nicholas and Smike are told the story by Mr. Vincent Crummles. Mr.

Crummles recited, *["the blood of the murdered man had run drop by drop into the hollow which gives the place its name". The Devil's Punch Bowl, thought Nicholas as he looked into the void, never held fitter liquer than that.].* We will learn more of the unfortunate sailor later on our walk.

The few honest people who braved to live in such a shunned area were mainly broom makers and wool spinners. Yet another writer, Mr. Baring Gould, based his novel "The Broom Squire" on the broom makers at the Punch Bowl and in it he captured perfectly the many moods of the surrounding heathland. Hopefully, you too unlike the early writers, will appreciate the beauty of your surroundings and of the Punch Bowl itself, whose mood and colours change dramatically with the seasons. The walk takes you around the perimeter of the Punch Bowl but I hope afterwards or on another day, you will make the effort to descend into the Bowl itself, where contrary to early superstition, you will find a sparkling stream which rises from a spring in the Bowl and escapes through Highcomb Bottom, gathering strength to eventually flow proudly into the river Wey. A dense vegetation of alder, willow, holly and oak covers the floor of the Bowl with numerous ferns providing the carpet.

If you are a keen botanist your interest will be taken by all the normal greensand flowers and a few of the rarer varieties such as the bog pimpernel, sneezewort, and skull-cap. Sneezewort incidentally, a plant from the daisy family, is probably so called because of powder made from the plant that was sometimes used as a form of snuff. Ornothologists too will not be disappointed, as numerous species of birds shelter in the Punch Bowl's protected environment. Humans also, contrary to the superstitions of years ago, have taken advantage of this sheltered haven. Several cottages dot the floor of the Punch Bowl, two of which have been converted into a Youth Hostel for those who wish to experience the simpler things in life (don't expect flush toilets!). One other, my favourite, almost in its original condition, is called "Gnome Cottage" - a fitting description and a name that is in keeping with the many dubious tales that once protected the secrets of the Bowl.

Sneezewort

The views from our vantage point are quite stunning, especially so in late summer when the Bowl becomes a rich shade of purple through blooming heathers. On the far rim is a distinct knoll with a sandy path over its summit, which is part of our return route. From the view point, follow the path past the memorial to shortly rejoin the track followed earlier and turn right along the track which soon begins to descend. Sometime later, the track again meets up with the line of telegraph poles mentioned earlier and runs parallel with them before eventually bending sharp right to descend into the Punch Bowl. There are two more tracks atthis point, one off to the left and another going straight on and beside them stands a wooden post marked with four blue arrows denoting that all routes are bridleways. You should leave the main track here (do not go downhill), and continue straight on along a well used bridleway, which continues to run through woodland, this time mainly oak and sweet chestnut with only the occasional ash.

24

After a short distance, ignore a path off to the right beside a post and blue arrow and carry straight on to begin a gradual descent. You will soon be walking between banks lined by holly bushes which, after passing a National Trust sign on the left, become much steeper and where in wet weather the going underfoot can be very muddy. Stay on the bridleway running between banks for approximately half a mile, to eventually lead out onto a track. This in turn leads to a lane, signposted as Hyde Lane.

Turn left along the lane to soon pass the beautiful "Upper Ridgeway Farm" complete with a small duck pond and after the farm, follow the lane downhill to shortly meet a track on your right marked with a red arrow. Take this, thereby leaving the lane and continue to soon pass over an often muddy crossing track which joins two fields. Soon after, when the track forks, take the right hand fork to descend, with the track narrowing into a path to run between banks. This later leads out onto a prominent track where you should continue ahead to pass a number of properties on your right, before arriving at a road.

Cross the road and then turn left to follow it in the direction of a blue arrow also marked by the letters "HR". After approximately two hundred and seventyfive metres and after the last house on your right, "March Hares", take a signposted public bridleway right, also marked by a blue arrow and "HR". You are now about to traverse army land where a sign here explains that this is army training ground and warns against touching suspicious objects. It also warns about the fact that as troops are regularly training here, there may be sudden movement and noises near the bridleway, so I hope your nerves are good. Essentially, you should keep to the marked bridleways and paths at all times and do not be tempted to wander.

Follow the bridleway which almost immediately climbs uphill through silver birch and pine and after a short distance, ignore a wide crossing track to continue ahead. Sometime later, go over two further crossing tracks and stay on the bridleway, still following the blue arrows. Go over the hill summit and then descend the other side to soon go over another wide crossing track. You will now follow a narrow bridleway downhill, still marked by the familiar blue arrows, though no longer marked with "HR".

As the bridleway descends it follows the left hand bank of a ditch, probably the original route, and sometime on, another path joins from the left which you should ignore to carry straight on. The woodland surrounding you now is almost entirely made up of pine and very different to that of Highcomb Copse. Stay on the bridleway ignoring any further turnings off and continue to eventually leave the woodland and arrive at an area of open heather, a real picture in late summer being a sea of vibrant purples and mauves. At the same time, you will meet a crossing track which you should ignore to carry straight on.

Sometime on, you will meet another crossing track which runs up a ridge on your right. As before, you should ignore this to carry straight on, once more entering pine woodland. (Ignore another track on your left as you join). As you progress, the bridleway begins to climb and you should follow it uphill, ignoring all turnings off and crossing tracks, to eventually meet a wide track at the top of the ridge, Kettlebury Hill. Turn left along the track in the direction of a blue arrow marked once again with an "HR" and continue along the ridge. As you progress further, there are superb views left across Frensham Common to Alice Holt Forest.

Follow the ridge in the direction of the blue arrows and ignore a track which descends off to your left. Soon after, pass a concrete pill box on your right and at the same time, ignore a number of tracks off to your left and right respectively to maintain your route. As you continue, the views on your right will open out across a heather covered basin to the wooded Houndown. The track forks at this point and you should take the right hand fork. As a guide, now visible and nestling below in the basin to your right, are some army buildings.

Stay on the track which continues to run along the top of the ridge, which now curves gently right and ignore any further turnings off. Apart from a few army buildings below, there are virtually no signs of any human habitation in any direction and it is very hard to believe that you are walking through Surrey. Eventually, you will arrive at a track which forks off to the left and is marked by a wooden post and blue arrow, as well as the number "108". Take this thereby leaving the hill top, to descend and arrive at a large junction of sandy tracks known as Lion's Mouth. Turn first right here along a track marked by a blue bridleway arrow and the number "101".

Immediately after joining, the track forks and you should take the right hand fork, a very sandy track which descends gradually running between banks and rhododendron bushes. The track then meets a lane. Turn left along the lane which almost immediately bends right to lead uphill. Follow it uphill where on reaching the top there is a car park on your right (alternative start). Our route is past the car park along the lane, unless you wish to avoid lane walking, in which case you should take a track here which runs parallel to the lane on your left (you will however, have to rejoin the lane when a wide track joins sometime later from the left).

Follow the lane, ignoring all turnings off to eventually arrive at a "T" junction beside a house on your left (**OS. 896407**). Cross the road and turn left to follow it, passing the entrance to "Truxford Riding Centre" on your left. A few paces on, the road bends left and you should leave it here to take a track right, signposted as a public bridleway. Immediately after joining, ignore another track off to the left and carry straight on to pass a house on your right. After the house, the track follows the line of some fields on your right and a strip of woodland on the left.

Sometime on, ignore another track right which leads into a field and continue along the track you have been following, keeping right, and following the perimeter of a field on your right. You will soon meet a crossing path, marked as a public bridleway. Turn right along the path in the direction of the blue arrow and continue to follow the line of the fields on your right. As you progress, the bridleway like so many others on this route, begins to run between banks and at the same time, becomes extremely sandy under foot.

As the fields on your right end, the bridleway forks and you should take the left hand fork, another bridleway, again marked by a blue arrow. This runs through the centre of a small wood (part of the large Thursley Nature Reserve), predominantly silver birch and oak and as before, you should follow the main path and ignore any turnings off to the left or right. After passing through an area of open bracken you will reach a prominent crossing track which you should cross to continue straight on, still following the blue arrows. A few paces on, you will meet another crossing path with a post which has a confusing number of blue arrows. As before, you should ignore this and go over the crossing path to continue your route ahead.

26

The path soon bends right to follow a hedge on your left and shortly arrives at a garden to a house on your right. Carry straight on, still following the hedge, to arrive at a road beside the beautiful "Vean Cottage". The cottage is one of many with equal beauty which make up the village of Thursley. If your timing is good, you will have reached Thursley during normal licencing hours and you may prefer to learn all about Thursley in the comfort of the excellent village hostelry, "The Three Horseshoes". The pub is reached by making a short detour left along the road, a route you will have to retrace to continue our walk.

Thursley (OS. 902397 Map 186). *This beautiful village is basically laid out in the shape of a "T". It demonstrates the changing tide of transport, for Thursley has always, until recently, been a stop-over for travellers taking long journeys on routes which passed through or close to the village. The original route was a drovers road which, leading past the church, formed the High Street and went on to the Devil's Punch Bowl. Later, priorities changed with the transport of people becoming more important than sheep and the modern day A3 became the major route, carrying coaches from London to the dockyards at Portsmouth.*

Thursley was a popular place to stay, especially as not stopping here usually involved traversing Hindhead Common at night. "The Red Lion" was constructed on the A3 to take advantage of this trade and became famous as the last drinking place of the unfortunate sailor, who was murdered on the common in the 18th century. Unfortunately (and probably because of the slight re-routing of the A3), "The Red Lion" no longer continues its trade. The same fate befell another pub in the village which, although protected from the fumes and the noise of the main road less than half a mile away, lost the benefit of trade that such a route brings.

Another equally well known but more fortunate traveller who stayed at Thursley was William Cobbett. Cobbett liked the village and wrote fondly of it though he would do his utmost to avoid visiting via Hindhead Common and would often divert for miles to achieve this. Two acacia trees grow on the village green and were presented in memory of Cobbett's visits, by Lieutenant Colonel Rushbrooke in 1934.

Over the centuries, apart from trade based on travellers, Thursley's two other main industries were glass blowing and iron working. The glass industry halted after strong and resentful competition from works at Guildford. Thursley's iron workings were based just north of the village and a number of dammed hammers ponds still exist today just west of the A3. Water from the ponds drove a water wheel which worked bellows and a large hammer, that in turn would crush iron stone. The iron industry brought great prosperity to Surrey but reduced dramatically when the Government discovered that locally made guns and amunition were being smuggled to Britain's arch enemy, France. In the mid-18th century there was also considerable unrest at the number of trees being felled for the iron furnaces and when it was found that coal could be used instead of wood, the death toll sounded for the Surrey iron industry. A third industry and one connected to the hammer ponds, was fish farming. After the Reformation the Government made it compulsory to eat fish on three days of the week, a decision based not just on religious but also very much upon economic grounds. When the iron works closed the fish industry became vital as a means of employment as well as feeding the local population. The industry still continues today in the form of a trout farm.

The name Thursley is derived from the Danish God of Thunder, Thor, and literally means "Thor's field" or "clearing", "Ley" being an early word for field and the reason why so many village and town names end in "ly" or "ley". Thor was probably simply a local Dane who took his name from his god. However, over the years, legends have grown up involving the god and not far away at the Devil's Jumps on Frensham Common, Thor is said to have felled the Devil with a giant stone. Place names too have evolved from some of the legends, a good example being Thunder Hill near Elstead. The village proudly displays its link with Thor and the god is featured on both the village and pub signs. The pub, "The Three Horseshoes", is a cosy affair with a respected restaurant. It is attached to the Gales Brewery at Horndean whose excellent beers are brewed using the spring water from Butser Hill in Hampshire.

As you pass through the village take an appreciative look around. There are many interesting old houses, one in particular near the pub has some interesting carvings on its chimney and another by the village green was once the home of the respected architect, Sir Edward Lutyens.

From "Vean Cottage", cross the road and join another road ahead, the other side of the small village green, signposted as The Street, leading to Highfield Lane and Thursley Parish Church. It is also a "No Through Road". Follow The Street (once the old drovers road), through the village of Thursley passing on the way a number of picturesque cottages and as you progress, look out for a track on your right signposted as a public footpath. Take this to run between houses and after the last house on the left, take a narrow path forking left off the main track, which runs around the perimeter of the house to enter the church yard. Continue ahead, passing to the left of the church and take time to enjoy the peaceful view across the graveyard on your left to the rooftops of Thursley village. You will shortly arrive at the church entrance in front of a beautiful old manor house.

The Church of St. Michael and All Angels, Thursley (OS. 901394 Map 186) *is of Saxon origin, built when the manor of Thursley was held by Godwin, Earl of Wessex and father of the ill-fated King Harold. The Victorians did their utmost to ruin the character of the church during so-called restorations but even so, it still* *retains some unique Saxon features. Most important, in 1927 the Vicar at the time discovered two perfect Saxon windows. They are situated in the north wall of the chancel and are the only ones in England to have their original timber frames. The other main feature which is immediately apparent, is the tower. This is unusual in as much as it is at the centre of the nave and is supported by an intricate system of huge timber beams. These were added to support the tower around the time of Henry VIII and are the best example of their type to be found in Surrey. Outside, the tower has a traditional sundial with an inscription in latin, "An hour is part of life".*

The church has continued to be well used over the centuries and during the second World War became a welcome place of worship for Canadian troops, stationed nearby. Later, between 1950 and 1955, the church welcomed Polish lutherans in exile. The churchyard is just as interesting. As you leave the church, look out for a gravestone to Richard Court on the left of the path which leads to the main gate. Richard Court was the village blacksmith who died in 1791. His epitaph recalls his valuable work,

> *" My sledge and hammer lie reclined,*
> *My bellows too have lost their wind,*
> *My fire is out and forge decay'd,*
> *And in the dust my vice is laid."*

From the church door, continue in a clockwise direction around the church and when the graveyard perimeter extends left (west), you should follow it to shortly go up a bank and continue between hedges. First though, take a look at the gravestone, known as the "Sailor's Stone", of the "Unknown Sailor" which is on the northern side of the churchyard facing the war memorial cross. The view from this part of the churchyard is superb, overlooking fields donated to the National Trust in honour of John Freeman, a poet and critic during the 1920's. His headstone is near to the churchyard wall, just to the right of the Sailor's Stone.

The Unknown Sailor*. The story of the unknown sailor is probably the most well known and most recited tale involving Thursley and Hindhead. It is sadly also the most tragic. The stone was errected through public subscription and a roughly carved picture and an unusual epitaph recall the sailor's violent end,*

> *"When pitying eyes to see my grave shall come,*
> *And with a generous tear below my tomb;*
> *Here shall they read my melancholy fate,*
> *With murder and barbarity complete.*
> *In perfect health and in the flower of age,*
> *I fell a victim to three ruffians' rage;*
> *On bended knees I mercy strove t'obtain,*
> *Their thirst of blood made all entreaties in vain.*
> *No dear relation or still dearer friend,*
> *Weeps my hard lot or miserable end;*
> *Yet o'er my sad remains (my name unknown),*
> *A generous public have inscribed this stone."*

The tragic day was 24th September, 1786 and the sailor was travelling the Portsmouth Road to join his ship. Like most other sailors, he would regularly stop at inns en route to enjoy some liquid refreshment. It was also common to meet fellow travellers at the inns before crossing Hindhead Common with a view to traversing the common in the safety of numbers. Unfortunately, this time the plan backfired. The sailor met some travelling companions at an inn at Mousehill, just outside Godalming. They were also sailors, Michael Casey, Edward Lanigan and James Marshall. It is said that one of the three claimed to be an old shipmate of the sailor, but it has since been suggested that this was a rouse to gain the confidence of their intended victim.

From the inn at Mousehill the four travelled to "The Red Lion" at Thursley, where the lone sailor paid for his companions drinks. That was the last time he was seen alive. Whilst traversing Hindhead Common the sailor's new found companions jumped him, killing him with multiple stab wounds which included cutting his throat so thoroughly, that they almost severed the head from his body. They then tipped his mutilated body over the edge of the Punch Bowl where they obviously thought it would not be discovered for days. Unfortunately for them, the body did not roll far and two men travelling not far behind noticed it in the moonlight and raised the alarm.

The three men were arrested in a pub at Sheet near Petersfield. All three pleaded guilty to their crime and were sentenced to be hanged. The hanging took place at the scene of their crime near the summit of the then to be called Gibbet Hill on Hindhead Common. Incidentally, did you know that the expression "hangers on" is dervied from this form of justice. Often the condemned person's weight was not enough to complete the throttle and young children would be paid half a penny to hang from the legs of the guilty party. They became known as "hangers on" and started an expression which was to become a common part of the English language. There is no evidence to suggest that this happened at Hindhead.

After the hanging, the bodies of the three men were cut down and tarred before being put in irons. Unfortunately, these did not fit and had to be altered at the forge at Thursley, probably by Richard Court whose gravestone I mentioned earlier. The mutilated body of the poor sailor was buried where you are standing and a shocked parish paid for the gravestone. It is a pity that such a beautiful area is so often only remembered for this tragic story.

Returning to our route, as mentioned, leave the churchyard by going up a bank and continuing between hedges. This naturally progresses into a footpath, which runs between a hedge on your right and a fence on the left and is now part of the Greensand Way. The footpath continues to soon run between fields and is intersperced by a number of stiles which you should cross to maintain your route, the last stile leading into a field. Once in the field, go diagonally right across the centre to reach and cross a stile beside a gate at the far side. Thereafter, go down a bank to very quickly arrive at a semi tarmacced lane in front of "Smallbrook Barn and Studio". Turn left along the lane, also marked as a public footpath, to immediately go uphill and follow it until it bends right. Here you should leave the lane and continue straight on along a wide path which runs between banks. The banks and the path soon bend left between fences and a yellow arrow marked with the letters "GW" here, indicates that you are still following the Greensand Way. There are good views left at this point to the Hogs Back.

You will soon arrive at a stile which you should cross to enter a field. Immediately after, turn right to follow the right hand perimeter of the field and at the far side, go over a stile and continue in the same direction along the right hand perimeter of the next field. As before, at the field end, go over a stile and continue ahead along a fenced path which follows the line of the next field. At the field end, the path bends left to follow the perimeter of "Hedge Farm". Again, you will meet and should cross another stile, after which you should follow the perimeter of the farm round to soon pass between the farmhouse on the right and some outbuildings on your left and arrive at the farm drive. Continue ahead along the drive and pass through a gate to meet a lane **(OS. 897388).**

Turn right along the lane and follow it as it almost immediately bends left, ignoring a signposted footpath off to the right. The lane eventually forks in front of a small green, at the middle of which stands a footpath sign and a sign for "Punch Bowl Farm". Take the left hand fork to continue ahead and pass a beautiful old farmhouse on your left. After the farmhouse the lane turns into a track and proceeds in a straight line between banks, topped by holly and beech trees. After approximately half a mile, the track forks in front of a National Trust sign where you should take the right hand fork to continue straight on.

Shortly after, the track forks again. This time you should take the left hand fork to soon pass over a crossing track and thereafter, climb uphill to re-enter the beautiful woodland of Hindhead Common. Continue along the track ignoring any turnings off to the left or right and follow it along the eastern rim of the Punch Bowl with familiar views over the Punch Bowl, this time in the opposite direction. Sometime on, pass a farm gate and stile on your right and shortly after, take a narrow path on your right which at first runs parallel to the track. Take care not to miss it. The path leads up the side of a distinct knoll, so prominent at our earlier view point on the western rim. The knoll (236m/774ft), probably affords the best views in Surrey, even better than Gibbet Hill which we visit shortly and is over 120 feet higher.

From the top of the hill, follow the path down the other side to soon meet the original track. Turn right along the track and head towards the very busy A3. Pass under a green barrier and ignore a marked bridleway off to the right and continue with care to cross the A3 and join a wide track the other side marked by a red arrow. This was the original coaching route from London to Portsmouth.

The A3. *Being a walker, I like many others resent the intrusion of bigger and faster roads eating into the easily developed countryside. Therefore, it may seem strange that I should choose to talk about a road and a main one at that. The A3 though has, I believe, a history worth telling and plays a major role in the history of Hindhead Common.*

It was the development of Portsmouth into a major naval base at the end of the 17th century that saw the rapid growth of the A3. Coaching inns sprang up at regular intervals along the way, sometimes with communities growing up around them. The original coaches started from the Elephant and Castle in London and would take fourteen hours (if they made it at all), to reach Portsmouth. These would often carry sailors (like our unfortunate friend), drinking their way from coaching inn to coaching inn turning many of the tranquil villages into noisy hell holes. Monies being spent on drink, the inn keepers and farmers would often allow the sailors to sleep in their barns or stables at a reduced rate. One can only imagine the smell when a crew after several days of drinking and sleeping in stables, rejoined their ship!

Over the years the road improved and towards the end of the 19th century, a coach could do the journey from London to Portsmouth in under ten hours. At this time, there were no less than twentyfour coaches a day operating the route. The road over Hindhead Common had always been considered treacherous and improvements in

1826, meant diverting it from going over the top of the hill to follow the rim of the Punch Bowl, which is still the route of the A3 we know today. Plans however, are afoot to divert it again to avoid congestion at Hindhead itself. These include a proposal to build a viaduct across the Punch Bowl which would completely destroy the wild aspect of the common, although as this book is published, the Department of Transport have put forward a much more agreeable plan involving a tunnel.

Standing on the track, the original coaching route, try and imagine yourself hundreds of years ago making your way across the common on a dark winter's night. There would have been no lights at Hindhead, no re-assuring sounds of car engines and bushes may have hidden highwaymen or simply desparate men willing to cut your throat for your clothes. As you approach the top of the hill, the bushes disappear and you are confused by a multitude of tracks. Without the protection of the undergrowth, the wind whips up the snow creating bitter conditions. You can now better understand peoples' reluctance to cross the common alone or at night. Many who tried regretted it later, getting lost, robbed or falling victim to the exposed conditions like a sailor, simply remembered as Samuel, who in 1778 was found dead on the road having perished from the cold. Eight years later of course, another sailor suffered a different but equally tragic fate. If these tales tempt you to hitchhike rather than cross the summit on foot, think again - the one ghost that haunts the hill is said to drive a black saloon car!

The track leads gently uphill, at first running parallel with the A3. Sometime later, ignore another track off to the right and stay on the track enjoying views which open out on your right across to the Punch Bowl, albeit which disappear just as quickly behind trees.

After approximately three quarters of a mile, the track forks in front of a post marked with three blue arrows at its top. Take the left hand fork here and follow a track away from the A3 and after a few paces, turn right onto a crossing path to pass between some wooden railings. You will now follow a narrow footpath uphill which soon arrives at an open grass and heather hill top, marked more definitely by a triangulation point and stone cross. Welcome to Gibbet Hill.

i

A cross marks the place where the Gibbet once stood

Gibbet Hill (OS. 900359 Map 186) *is a recent name given after the three murderers were hung in chains from a gibbet at the summit here. The stone Iona cross donated by Sir William Earl in 1831, marks the spot where the gibbet stood. The gibbet acted as a grizly reminder to the murder until 23rd December, 1790 when a storm blew it down. Another stone, not at the summit, marks the spot where the murder took place. An inscription on the back reads, "Cursed be the man who injureth or removeth this stone". Despite this, the stone was moved from its original position to the site of the current A3. There are reports that those involved died shortly after, but these cannot be verified. Later, the stone was returned to its original position where it still stands today.*

Moving to a more pleasant subject, the views from the summit (895ft) and the highest point on our walk, are quite spectacular. On the triangulation point, a brass direction finder helps identify major landmarks, though be prepared for these to be hidden in the low cloud or mist which freqently enshrouds the hill. Whatever the weather, I suggest you take advantage of one of the conveniently sited benches for a well deserved rest before the last and easy home stretch to our starting point.

To continue, carry straight on across the hill top passing between the triangulation point and the stone cross. Soon after, you will enter an area surrounded by banks, probably once used as a car park. At the other side, three tracks leave the parking area. You should take the left hand track passing to the left of a wooden post, to continue straight on. Thereafter, follow the track through picturesque oak woodland and continue to shortly arrive at another junction of tracks.

Ignore all turnings off at the junction and carry straight on along the main track to meet a fork. Take the right hand fork which runs gently downhill to meet a "T" junction in the form of a wide track beside a seat on your right. Turn right along the track ignoring a narrower path which runs behind the seat and follow the track as it soon crosses open heathland. The views left now are across to the South Downs and before them, Woolbeding Common, featured in "10 Adventurous Walks in West Sussex". Also visible is Butser Hill in Hampshire.

Stay on the track, ignoring all turnings off, to eventually arrive at a timber yard belonging to the National Trust. Pass through the timber yard to soon meet the noisy A3, which certainly needs no introduction. To your left here is "The Devil's Punch Bowl Hotel". You simply now have to cross the A3 to reach our starting point where you may wish to take time for a snack at the cafe in the car park, although a much nicer treat as long as your appearance after the walk allows, is a drink and perhaps a meal at "The Devil's Punch Bowl Hotel".

Hindhead and The Devil's Punch Bowl Hotel (OS. 887357 Map 186). *Until 1887, Hindhead was simply a few cottages and an hotel, "The Royal Huts Hotel". Things changed abruptly when a leading physicist, John Tyndell, built a house here claiming the fresh air and scenery was as good as Bel Alp in Switzerland, where the well established travelled to improve their health. Being well known in society, Tyndell started a trend and soon Hindhead was being developed for its famous new residents, who included the novelist George Elliot, Sir Arthur Conan-Doyle of Sherlock Holmes fame who built a house which he called "Undershaw", now an hotel and Lord Methuen and Lord Beveridge. George Bernard-Shaw was another who moved here, to a house called "Blen Cathra", now a school.*

Shops and hotels sprang up and at this time, "The Devil's Punch Bowl Hotel" was built as a country residence for the Honourable Rollo Russell, who was the son of Lord John Russell, England's first Liberal Prime Minister. The house then called "Thorshill", was later leased to a Reverend Alfred Kluht, who with his wife ran the house as a guest house to help pay the rent. The house has welcomed visitors ever since. Hindhead's original hotel nicknamed "The Huts", has now been converted to a fast-food restaurant and motel.

The original coaching route still transports travellers through the centre of Hindhead. No doubt local residents will be pleased when this is diverted, but I cannot help feeling that when it is Hindhead will lose forever a living part of its history and with it some of its character.

If you have enjoyed your walk and the many secrets en route, then I hope you will pay a visit on another day to explore the area more fully.

ACCOMMODATION

The Devil's Punch Bowl Hotel, Hindhead. Tel: 0428 606565
On the walk, this distinctive hotel was built as a country residence for the
Honourable Rollo Russell. The hotel is a convenient and comfortable place to stay,
with all rooms having en suite facilities. It offers some good packages and welcomes
walkers.

Little Cowdray Farm, Thursley. Tel: 0428 605016
On the walk, this is a delightful place to stay. The farm is situated on the old
drovers road south of Thursley. It is only a short walk to the National Trust owned
Hindhead Common and not much further to The Three Horseshoes at Thursley.

**Youth Hostel, Hindhead YHA, Devil's Punch Bowl, Hindhead.
Tel: 0428 734285**
Virtually on the walk, this is a simple youth hostel situated in the bowl of the
Devil's Punch Bowl. Basic but idyllic, I found my stay here a welcome break from
the 20th century. Camping is also permitted amongst the rabbits!

Camping & Caravanning, Tilford Touring, Tilford. Tel: 025125 3296
One mile from the walk, this site is in a particularly pleasant setting surrounded by
Hankley Common, within walking distance of the Duke of Cambridge pub at
Tilford. The site is open all year round.

THE NAVIGATORS WAY

Distance: 10 miles (16 km)
Time: Allow approximately 5 hours
Map: Ordnance Survey Landranger Map 186

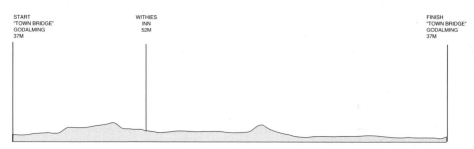

START
"TOWN BRIDGE"
GODALMING
37M

WITHIES
INN
52M

FINISH
"TOWN BRIDGE"
GODALMING
37M

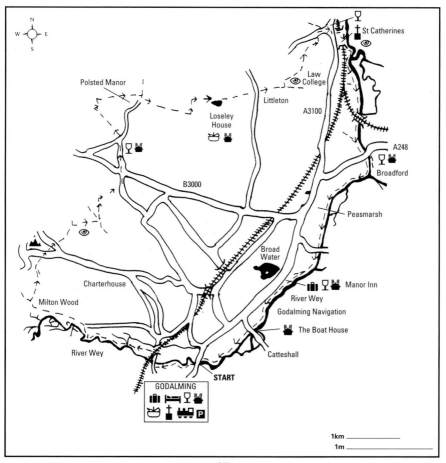

35

Walk Summary
This is a beautiful walk achieved with relatively little effort. The going at all times
is fairly easy and yet the route passes through some beautiful countryside, with the
highlight being the towpath along the river Wey Navigation. Apart from the
glorious countryside and its wildlife, the walk has a wealth of other interests and
you will discover some magnificent buildings which have survived the test of time.
As a finale, you can give your feet a rest and take a boat trip along the river.

Start - OS. 973442 Map 186
The walk starts from the A300 in front of the town Library and beside the Town
Bridge at Godalming. To clarify, the Library is situated between the river Wey and
the old United Reform church, now an auction room, at the northern end of town.
There are a number of car parks in town, none of them being more than a few
minutes walk from the Library.

Getting to Godalming by car is easy, with it being on or close to a number of "A"
roads, including the A3 from where the town is signposted. Godalming also has a
railway station which is on the main Waterloo to Portsmouth line. From the station
it is no more than a five minute walk to the Library, our starting point. There is no
obvious alternative start.

THE NAVIGATORS WAY

Whether you arrive to start the walk by car, train, bus or even on foot, you will
probably have to pass through part of Godalming to reach our starting point.
Therefore, I feel it is worth knowing a little about what is, in my opinion, one of the
most pleasant towns in Surrey, though I suggest you try the hostelries I recommend
after the walk and not before!

Godalming (OS. 970439 Map 186) *has an idyllic setting nestling in a sleepy river
valley surrounded by perfectly rounded hills. If you are one of the people who has
always bypassed Godalming on the way to somewhere else, then you are about to be
pleasantly surprised. Off of the picturesque High Street, a testament to Godalming's
prosperous past, lie narrow streets of half timbered cottages and cosy pubs.*

*Although neolithic and iron age remains have been discovered all around
Godalming, it is believed that the town itself is of Saxon origin. What is certain is
that the name is derived from a Saxon, Godhelm, probably a Chieftain and
Godalming literally translated means, "Godhelm's field". Later, Godalming was to be
owned by that great Saxon King, Alfred, who left it in his will to Ethelwald. It was
about this time that the present church was built.*

*Godalming slowly grew in prosperity and was given a significant boost when in 1300,
Edward I granted the town the right to hold a weekly market and a three day annual
fair. The right to hold a market was very important in the Middle Ages and virtually
guaranteed prosperity to the town. In 1574, the town received another boost when
Elizabeth I granted Godalming a Charter enabling it to control its own affairs. The
modern equivalent would be the formation of a borough run by a council. The one
anomaly of the Charter was that the control of land sales and planning permission
was not given to the town, but to the powerful More family at Loseley (visited later on
the walk), who retained this privilege right up until the end of the last century.*

*Godalming's real wealth however, came with the rise of the wool industry. From the
Middle Ages right up until the 18th century, Godalming was the centre of the*

clothing industry in Surrey and many of the town's magnificent buildings came as a direct result of the wealth created by this trade. With the demise of the wool and cloth industry many clothing based towns virtually collapsed, but fortunately for Godalming came the rise of the Portsmouth dockyard and the consequential coaching route to London which passed through the town. This brought its own trade and a few years later a second saviour, the opening of the river Wey to Godalming for industrial traffic, created yet more wealth for the town. This was mostly used for the paper and timber industries, Godalming taking advantage of being virtually surrounded by extensive woodland.

More recently, Godalming was the pioneer of an industry which has now become an essential part of everyday life. In 1881 Godalming became the first town in the world to have electric street lighting. At first, just three street lamps were lit, with power generated from a water wheel at one of Godalming's tanning mills. This used a system developed by Siemens. Such was the success of this venture that soon the whole High Street was lit and other towns quickly followed.

The people of Godalming were not so quick however, to endorse another invention, the motor car. The turn of the century saw the rapid development of the motor car and its power and speed greatly alarmed the local council, who became notorious for rigorously enforcing the national speed limit of five miles per hour! At this time, the law was enforced by a man walking in front of the vehicle carrying a red flag. In 1903, the speed limit was raised to ten miles per hour and the red flag system was abolished. Not to be daunted, the council employed its men in setting up speed traps and Godalming became a place to be avoided (nothing changes!). Eventually, after protests from local traders, the council relaxed their position and cars returned to Godalming's High Street. Today, the council may be called "visionary", as a far more expensive action in the building of a bypass has now removed the motor car once again from the High Street.

Godalming has many buildings of interest and far too many to include here. There are however, two (aside of the pubs to be recommended) which cannot be ignored. The first is the old Town Hall, affectionately known as "The Pepper Pot", which is a dominant feature of the High Street. From this spot it is known that the town's affairs have been administered for over one thousand years, an incredible record. The current building dates from 1814 and replaced a Tudor building which also housed the town's dungeon and stocks. Cellars belonging to the "The Red Lion" opposite, used to house additional prisoners when the town's dungeons were full. Evidently, the dungeon was preferable as two prisoners once drowned when the pub cellars flooded. The second building, is the church which overlooks the river. Despite being heavily restored in the 19th century, the church has kept many original features.

Buildings apart, Godalming has produced some notable people. Perhaps the most famous is James Oglethorpe, who went on to found the state of Georgia, U.S.A., in 1732. Another resident of the 18th century, equally famous locally but for nothing so worthwhile, was Mary Tofts, better known as the Rabbit Woman. She became famous for claiming to give birth to a litter of rabbits. Perhaps her claim would not have been taken seriously but she was supported by a local doctor and a surgeon appointed by the King. After further investigations, Mary Tofts predictably was declared a fraud and Godalming became the butt of rabbit jokes, travellers often hopping along the streets or making cat noises. I would advise that for your own safety you do not follow suit!

Finally and most important to most of you, are the town's hostelries of which Godalming can boast plenty. Most are centred around the High Street. "The Kings Arms and Royal Hotel", Hospitality Inns, is the most famous and as its name suggests, has been host to royalty in its time. The most notable of these was Tsar Peter the Great who stayed here in 1698. From all accounts his and his party's behaviour was equal to today's football hooligans. An example of their sheer gluttony was their bill for breakfast. Twentyone men devoured half a lamb, half a sheep, twentytwo fowl, eightyfour eggs, a gallon of brandy and a quart each of mulled wine. There are stories of several hauntings in the hotel which include the sounds of a noisy party, a distinct possibility that the Tsar and his friends have never left. The main bar which is panelled, is smart and comfortable but somehow lacks atmosphere - surprising for such an historic venue.

The best pubs for me are situated at the western end of the High Street near "The Pepper Pot" and the best of these, in my opinion, are "The Rose and Crown", Pheonix, "The Star", a free house, and "The Red Lion", Courage. All of the pubs date from or before the 18th century and all have a distinct atmosphere of their own. "The Rose and Crown" is probably my favourite, especially in summer when you can sit outside in the pub's cosy backyard, though beware of its female ghost. All the pubs mentioned serve food and they all serve excellent ales with regular guest beers - the people of Godalming must appreciate their ale!

To start the walk, take a tarmac footpath which passes to the right of the Library and left of the Town Bridge to, after a few paces, meet the river Wey where you should follow the footpath left, walking upstream. This takes you around behind the Library and continues parallel to a service road, The Burys, to Godalming town centre on your left. On the opposite bank the other side of a pleasant meadow, Lammas Lands, rises Frith Hill. The tower visible at the top is nothing more romantic than a water tower.

The path continues passing between some beautiful willow trees to shortly meet a bowling green. If you look across the river to the meadow at this point, you can just make out a shallow marshy hollow. This is where the public hanging of Chennell and Chalcraft took place.

i **Godalming's Last Public Hanging.** *On 11th November, 1817 the battered bodies of two harmless elderly people were discovered at their home. They were the father of George Chennell and Elizabeth Wilson, his housekeeper. Both had had their throats cut and had been hit about the head with a heavy instrument. Blatant evidence soon led to the arrest of George Chennell and his friend, William Chalcraft. Despite their continuing denials, the two were convicted of murder and sentenced to hanging. On 14th August, 1818 the two men were hanged in front of thousands of people who packed the meadows on both sides of the river and the slopes of Frith Hill. Both men repeated their innocence as the wagon, their last support, was driven off and the sentence carried out. The last public hanging at Godalming.*

After the bowling green the path forks and you should take the left hand fork and carry straight on, ignoring a crossing path to pass the parish church on your left. After a short distance, you will arrive beside the Phillips Memorial Cloister on the right.

i **The Phillips Memorial Cloister (OS. 968441 Map 186)** *remembers the tragic end of Jack Phillips. Mr. Phillips who was born at nearby Farncombe, had been appointed Chief Wireless Officer on board the SS Titanic and died with hundreds of* *others when it hit an iceberg on her maiden voyage, 13th April, 1912.*

After the memorial the path meets a road. Cross the road and turn right along a tarmac path (the lower path), which runs parallel to the pavement and road, to soon cross the river by way of a wooden footbridge. *This is called Boarden Bridge and for* **i** *centuries was the only bridge across the river at this end of the town. The road bridge, called the Lunatic Bridge (though not I'm told, because of the lunatic drivers that speed over it), is built over the old ford. Looking upstream beyond the railway bridge, you can just make out some modern industrial buildings. They replaced Westbrook Mills which generated the world's first street lighting.*

At the other side of the bridge you will arrive at a car park where you should **P** continue ahead, straight across the car park, ignoring the main exit on your right, to leave through a smaller exit the other side. Bear left thereafter, and follow the road under a railway bridge, immediately after which you should turn left onto a signposted footpath. This follows a fence on your left and an arm of the river Wey on your right and soon meets a road beside a security entrance to a modern industrial site on your left.

Cross the road and join a tarmac footpath the other side which goes over another arm of the river Wey to thereafter, follow the same earlier arm on your right. After a short distance, the footpath meets the river Wey itself and continues to follow it, albeit now on your left. Stay on the tarmac path, ignoring any turnings off, to later cross another arm of the river via a wooden footbridge. On your left at this point, is a pretty man-made waterfall which acts as an overflow.

Soon after, on meeting a seat on your right, leave the tarmac path and take a track which forks left, still following the river. Take care not to miss it. Stay on the track which meanders with the course of the river and follow it when sometime later, it bends right away from the river, passing to the left of a pill box. Immediately after, cross another arm of the Wey via a concrete bridge and follow the track gently uphill alongside a fence and garden on your right.

On meeting a lane at its end, turn left to follow a signposted footpath to Shackleford. This is a prominent path which follows a stone wall on the right.

Charterhouse. *The wall is the boundary to the grounds of the famous* **i** *Charterhouse School. The school was founded in 1611 at Smithfield in London from money left in the will of Sir Thomas Sutton. In 1872, the school which shared a building with Sutton hospital (also created as a result of Sutton's will), moved to Godalming which had a most valuable asset, space. The hospital incidentally, still continues its good work. The school buildings (not visible from this point), were designed by one Philip Hardwick and included a striking one hundred and fifty foot tower, known as Founders Tower. Over the years, Charterhouse has educated some of England's finest, including Addison, Thackeray and John Wesley. More recently, some members of the rock group Genesis benefited from a Charterhouse education.*

The school's other claim to fame is football. The school participated at the foundation meeting of the F.A. (Football Association), and later its old Carthusians side went on to win both the F.A. Cup and the F.A. Amateur Cup, the only team ever to do so.

The wall very quickly ends and your route continues through the beautiful Milton Wood, where to your left through the trees you will gain brief glimpses of the river Wey. After approximately half a mile, the footpath passes a lovely stone house on the left set in picturesque grounds and thereafter, passes through a small wooden gate to arrive at the main drive to the house. Continue straight on along the drive and after approximately fifty metres, turn right onto a marked bridleway which follows a stone wall on your left to another, this time much grander, house. Ignore a path leading off to the right which leads steeply uphill and stay on the bridleway, which runs gently uphill through fairly thick undergrowth or scrub.

Sometime later, ignore a signposted public footpath which joins from the right and continue ahead for another twenty paces or so until you meet a marked public bridleway on your right. Take this to begin a slightly steeper ascent and ignore any turnings off to later continue between hedges and arrive at a road. Cross the road and join a signposted public bridleway the other side, which is hedged and runs between gardens. On meeting another road, cross this (dangerous crossing) and join a tarmac drive the other side, again marked as a public bridleway.

Follow the drive until it bends right opposite "Broomfield Manor", where you should leave it to carry straight on along another drive. After a short distance, this forks to enter two properties. You should ignore the two drives and take a narrow path directly ahead, ignoring another off to the right. Follow the path downhill, passing one of the properties on your left, to soon pass through woodland. At the other side of the wood on meeting a field ahead, follow the path, still a bridleway, as it bends sharp right and ignore a footpath on the left **(OS. 956459)**.

The bridleway follows the perimeter of the field and affords lovely views across to the Hogs Back. On reaching the far side of the field, ignore some steps off to the right and a stile on the left, to stay on the bridleway as it bends left, still following the field perimeter. When the field on your left ends, follow the bridleway as it twists right to follow the right hand perimeter of another field. On reaching a track at the far side, turn left to follow it ignoring a white gate on the right.

Immediately after passing a house on your right, leave the field and join a bridleway on the right which runs between the field and the garden to the house mentioned. The bridleway soon rejoins the track, where you should turn right along it and ignore a marked crossing path to shortly reach a narrow lane in front of some pretty cottages which sit at the other side of a green. Turn left along the lane to soon arrive at a "T" junction, the road being the B3000. Cross the road and continue ahead along a path which cuts across a small grass area and meets Withies Lane. Turn left along the lane to now head for "The Withies Inn" which is signposted, passing a number of pretty houses and cottages which are part of the village of Compton.

"The Withies Inn" is a 16th century free house famous for its food. Inside, a magnificent carved oak bar dominates a small restaurant and snug lounge which still have many of the original features, including a huge inglenook fireplace. Unfortunately, most of the people who frequent the inn do so for its food and the bar tends to act as an extension to the restaurant, which means standing room only for the drinker. To compensate however, the inn serves a good and unusual selection of real ales. Outside, it has one of the best pub gardens I have come across, as much an attraction as the inn itself.

After "The Withies Inn" you will pass a pretty pond on the right and should continue to follow the lane as it later bends sharp left, ignoring another lane off to the right marked as a dead end. A few paces on, leave the lane and join a footpath on your right, passing over a stile to do so. The footpath initially follows the line of a field on your right and as this ends, it continues through a beautiful deciduous wood known as Bummoor Copse. You should ignore all turnings off and follow the footpath through the copse to eventually meet and cross a stile at the other side. This takes you into a field where you should carry straight on along the right hand perimeter.

At the far side of the field, go over a stile on your right and follow a fenced path around the perimeter of another field, where there are views left across to "Coney Croft Farm". Just before meeting a concrete drive to the farm, turn right over a stile and follow a fairly prominent path across a field, running parallel to a track on your left. After a short distance and just after passing a ditch on your right, leave the field by way of a stile on your left and continue thereafter, in the same direction, along a fenced footpath. This soon meets and follows the perimeter of a garden on your right and passes above the beautiful "Polsted Manor".

Soon after "Polsted Manor", follow the footpath down some steps to arrive at a "T" junction in the form of a sunken path. Turn right at the "T" junction and after a few paces, turn left onto a signposted public footpath in front of an entrance to "Little Polsted" and "Polsted Manor". The footpath, more a track, is hedged and runs between fields in an easterly direction.

Sometime later, pass "Polsted House", a gatehouse to Loseley Park, where you should pass through a kissing gate and continue ahead along the track. This soon runs through an avenue of horse chestnut trees, at the end of which it meets an adventure playground on the left. Go over a stile on your left here and follow a narrow path around the perimeter of Loseley Park. (N.B. Please take note of the "private" signs, although there is no gate here, this is not the official entrance to Loseley Park). Continue to meet and cross a second stile and as before, follow a narrow path ahead, this time along a magnificent line of oaks.

On meeting a stile on your left, cross this and turn immediately right to follow the right hand perimeter of a field. At the field corner, go over another stile, turn immediately left and after approximately twenty paces, go over a third stile, again on your left, into another field. Turn right after the stile and follow the perimeter of the field, enjoying views to your right across to "Loseley House".

Loseley House (OS. 975473 Map 186) *is one of the great houses of Britain and is still owned by the family that originally built it over four hundred years ago, the More's. The house was built in 1562 by Sir William More using stones from the nearby ruined Waverley Abbey. Sir William went on to become one of the main confidants to Elizabeth I and the Queen stayed at Loseley on more than one occasion. Later, King James I and Queen Mary were also to visit Loseley.*

One of the great romances of the 17th century took place at Loseley. Anne More, daughter of Sir George More, William's son, was wooed by her father's Secretary, one John Donne and in 1600 secretly married him. Donne was well respected and the Earl of Northumberland, a friend of Sir George, thinking he would be pleased, broke the happy news. Sir George who considered the marriage an insult, was furious and promptly not only sacked Donne but imprisoned him along with several other people who were closely involved with the wedding. There followed a series of passionate letters from all parties involved and eventually Donne was released and even managed to make his peace with Sir George. He later went on to become Dean of St. Paul's and a celebrated poet.

The male line of the More's died with Sir Robert More in 1689 and with the marriage

Loseley House

*of Margaret More to a member of the Molyneux family, the name More-Molyneux was
adopted, which is still used today. The house, which is open to the public (tel: 0483
304440 for opening times), has an atmosphere fitting with its role as a home to one of
the most powerful families the country has ever known. Still a home and lovingly
cared for by the present generation, the house is definitely not a museum. Instead,
passing through rooms unchanged over the centuries, rooms which have witnessed
action and conversations by people who shaped the history of our country, you cannot
help feeling grateful for the privilege of being allowed in. An inscription in latin over
the inner door of the entrance hall makes you feel a little better. It reads, "I am shut
to envy but always open to a friend".*

*Such a great house would not be complete without its ghosts and Loseley has several.
One ghost is said to be a lady in Victorian costume (origin unknown), another is a
woman and her child. The woman is said to have drowned her child in the moat which
once surrounded the house. The ghost of the family's most famous member, Sir Thomas
More, who was executed in 1535 before the house was built, is said to visit the house
every other year from his permanent haunting at Baynards Park, also in Surrey.*

At the far side of the field your route will naturally join a grass track, to continue in
the same direction and soon passes a beautiful lake on your right. After the lake the
track bends right and you should leave it here to go over a stile ahead. This takes you
into a field where you should continue ahead, across the centre, with views ahead to
your right of Blackheath and Pitch Hill. At the far side, go over a stile and carry
straight on across the next field and at the field end, go over yet another stile to cross
the centre of a third field. You should now be heading for some houses at the far side
which make up the hamlet of Littleton.

At the far side of the field, go over a stile beside a gate and continue ahead along a
track, passing a lovely house on your left and the old school, now a youth centre, on
your right. On reaching a lane beside a tiny telephone box, cross this to join a
narrow tarmac drive the other side. If however, you wish to visit "Loseley House",
you will need to detour right here, along the lane, to reach the entrance. You will
need to retrace your steps to rejoin our route.

The drive takes you past a number of pretty cottages and a grand house on the
right, after which you will pass a small bungalow on the same side where the drive
ends. You should carry straight on, now following a narrow path which runs
between fields and when the field on your left ends, you will meet a footpath off to
the left which you should take. On your right as you join are the grounds of Mount
Browne Police Headquarters, which also acts as a training establishment and
specialises in training police dogs. After a short distance, the path bends right and
starts to climb uphill, where you can enjoy views to your right of Chinthurst Hill

and the wooded landscape of west Surrey. The prominent church spire also in view belongs to the church of St. Mary the Virgin at Shalford. The churchyard was once the site of Shalford fair, said to have been the inspiration for Thackeray's "Vanity Fair". The path then continues to pass behind the main buildings of the Police College of Law to eventually arrive at a road.

Follow the road ahead for a few paces to meet a lane. Cross the lane and pass through a gap in a stone wall the other side, to join a narrow path ahead which soon meets another lane. Carry straight on here and follow the lane gently downhill where, after a short distance, you will pass a North Downs Way sign on the left. You should ignore this and stay on the lane, from here also part of the North Downs Way, to eventually meet a main road, the A3100, in front of "Ye Olde Ship Inn".

Cross the road and turn right to pass in front of the pub and soon arrive at Ferry Lane on your left. Cross Ferry Lane to take a grass path the other side, going up the side of St. Catherine's Hill. Do not make the mistake of taking the track which leads around the side of the hill, allowing access to a row of pretty cottages. At the top, are the remains of the famous St. Catherine's chapel. You will also achieve the best views on the walk, making this a perfect place for a rest.

St. Catherine's Chapel (OS. 994482 Map 186) *has a lofty position above the river Wey with good views over the Wey valley, Albury Downs and to Guildford and its Norman castle. The chapel was built in the 14th century by Richard de Wauncey, to provide a place of worship for parishioners who found the trip to the church at the centre of Guildford too much. Another reason and being a cynic, was, I believe, probably the main reason, namely that the chapel was built to obtain a licence to hold a fair on the hill. A fair could bring the licencee considerable wealth. The only person who could grant the licence was the King and chances of success were considerably greater if there was a religious connection. The licence was granted by Richard II in 1308. The chapel remained in use for just over two hundred years, but the fair continued into the 19th century.*

Legend links St. Catherine's with the Pilgrims Way which is supposed to have taken the route of Ferry Lane, below the hill. Arguments as to whether this route ever existed still continue today (see "In Pilgrims' Footsteps"), but one thing is certain, at the time when pilgrims were supposed to make their way to Canterbury, St. Catherine's Hill was bare.

From the front of the chapel facing the river Wey and the Albury Downs (facing east), you have the choice of two routes. Either continue ahead (east), along a narrow path which passes to the left of some fencing, after which you must scramble down a sandy cliff to the banks of the river Wey and turn right to follow the river. Alternatively, if scrambling is not your idea of fun, retrace your steps to Ferry Lane, to then follow it in the direction of the North Downs Way sign. Ferry Lane runs between houses and then over a railway line, which disappears into a tunnel at this point on your right and passes under St. Catherine's Hill. Thereafter, the lane goes sharply downhill between some more picturesque properties, my favourite being "Pilgrim Cottage" on the left. After "Pilgrim Cottage" a stream springs from beneath St. Catherine's Hill and an ornate stone bridge and seat have been added, creating a fairytale scene. Immediately after this you will arrive at the river Wey, where you should turn right in the direction of a footpath sign. You will shortly meet a bridge which you should ignore to continue along the river bank, thereby leaving the North Downs Way but joining another long distance route, the Wey South Path. Pass the base of the sandy cliff which is where the two alternative descents from St. Catherine's Hill now meet.

Follow the river which soon bends left where you will enjoy good views of the bridge just passed taking the North Downs Way across the river.

Sometime on, the river seemingly forks as the Tillingbourne joins from the east. You should ignore a footpath off to the right here and continue ahead, passing through a lovely area of open watermeadows. Thereafter, you will arrive at your first lock, St. Catherine's, where you should ignore a bridge across the lock as well as a stile off to the right. It was whilst resting at this lock that I saw my first mink swimming strongly from the opposite bank, a good opportunity I feel, to mention some of the wildlife you may encounter along the river.

i **Wildlife along the River Wey Navigation.** *Apart from the ever hungry ducks, the Wey valley is home to a wide variety of birds. Those which are easily spotted include the mute swan, the Canadian goose, the coote and the shy moorhen which lives close to the bank. Just as prevalent but not so easy to spot, are the grey heron and the kingfisher, the latter normally only seen as a dazzling flash as it skims the water in search of food. In summer, the air is alive with insects, chased at high speed by the ever alert swifts, house martins and swallows in pursuit of their next meal. The lush water meadows and surrounding woodland which cover the valley floor, are a natural habitat to the shyer birds, too numerous to mention here. In case you are lucky enough to spot one, I recommend you invest in a pocket book of birds.*

Dragon Fly

Three mammals which inhabit the banks of the river are the water shrew, the water vole and the mink. The water shrew is distinguishable by its black coat and white underbody. It feeds mainly on worms and small spiders but will take to the water to catch fish or even frogs. The water vole is much larger and has a brown coat. Its appearance means it is often mistaken for a rat and is commonly called a water rat. Unlike the water shrew, the water vole feeds almost entirely on waterside plants. Much rarer, but growing in population, especially along the river Wey, is the mink, now considered a naturalised British inhabitant. Minks were first introduced to Britain from North America in the 1920's for the fur trade. The wild minks in Britain today are the descendants of some of the luckier arrivals who escaped from the fur farms. They are particularly good swimmers and fish forms a large part of their staple diet.

This is just a short and very limited description of some of the wildlife along the Wey valley. For example, I have not mentioned frogs, toads and snakes, the latter being something that I spotted on the same day as my first sighting of a mink. Whilst walking along the towpath, a grass snake plunged into the river and swam across to the other bank to avoid being caught under my feet - a good precaution for both parties I thought! I have also barely mentioned the wealth of insect life such as the glamorous damsel and dragonflies which create such a regal display above the water. The rest must be left for you to discover. Tread carefully and keep your wits about you and you will be

Heron

rewarded by a display missed by many who use the towpath.

Continuing, stay on the river bank to later pass a house on the left and a small weir (which has the peculiar name of Riff-Raff), just after. A few metres on, pass under an iron railway bridge which carries the line between Guildford and Redhill and soon after, look out for a pill box, somewhat hidden in the trees on your right.

The Last Line of Defence. *This pill box was one of several thousand built in the 1940's to defend key points in Britain in case of invasion. This particular pill box was part of the last line of defence, defending London and the north of Britain and stretched from Chatham in Kent to Bristol. The pill boxes were so well constructed that it was too expensive for them to be demolished after the second World War. Today, they remain as an interesting but sombre reminder of those unsettled times.*

Kingfisher

i

Behind this pill box stretches an embankment which was intended to take the railway line from Redhill, south. The bridge and line were never completed and today the embankment serves as a footpath, though not part of our route.

The river continues through more open countryside before arriving at the next landmark, the green and white Broadford Bridge which carries a main road, the A428, over the river. A short detour left here over the bridge, will bring you to "The Parrot Inn". This is a friendly pub with one large bar and a restaurant housed in a conservatory which fronts the pub. In summer, you can take advantage of the large attractive garden.

Our route however, is across the A428 to join the towpath the other side, thereby continuing our walk along the right hand river bank but leaving the Wey South Path which continues from here along the left hand (eastern) bank of the river. The block of offices on the opposite bank are not unsightly and are indeed, an improvement on the previous buildings which housed a fibre works and gunpowder factory. After the offices, the river forks with the Wey and Arun canal leaving the river, left. After the gunpowder factory this junction became known as Guns Mouth. We now follow the Godalming Navigation and soon pass between the brick and concrete buttresses which once supported the former Horsham railway line. After the old bridge, the water meadows lining our route on the right are now overtaken by a pleasant wood, in the midst of which you may spot another old pill box.

i

Continue along the river bank to later pass over an old rickety wooden bridge which crosses an arm of the Godalming Navigation. The arm is on your right and is used mainly for mooring, but once led to Unstead Mill where working barges were loaded. Soon after the bridge, you will arrive at your second lock, Unstead Lock. At this point, the river passes a small industrial complex on your right, unimaginatively called "Riverside", after which it returns to more pastural surroundings. To your right, the other side of a field, you can see the pretty "Tiltham's Farm".

i

On reaching a lane which goes over the river, cross this to continue along the towpath the other side. You will now pass through one of the most pleasant parts of the walk, with the river cutting through picturesque water meadows which in turn are bordered by the wooded Farley Hill on the left. In places, where the water meadows on your right end, they are replaced by a line of attractive houses, after which you will pass "The Manor Inn", a Beefeater pub and restaurant. A short distance after "The Manor Inn", the river reaches one of the most attractive bridges on the route, which sits beside an equally attractive cottage on your right. Do not cross the bridge, but continue along the towpath.

At the next bridge on the river you will also arrive at "The Boathouse", which apart from housing a restaurant and cafe, offers canoes, skiffs and rowing boats for rent on the river. There are also longboats to get away for a weekend or longer. *Behind "The Boathouse", is an area known as Catteshall. This is an old name and means "hill of the wild cat" and has led to speculation that the area was once the domain of the so-called Surrey Puma, a huge wild black cat of which there are still regularly reported sightings.*

Cross the road here and maintain your route along the towpath the other side, which is now raised and runs parallel with a field on your right, the beginning of Lammas Lands. Later, you will pass the old Godalming Wharf on the far bank, now home to the Godalming Packetboat Company, which offers traditional horse-drawn narrow-boat trips. The towpath eventually ends at a car park beside Godalming United Church. Walk through the car park to meet the main road, the A3100, and turn left to follow it over the river via the Town Bridge. The bridge up until 1783 was privately owned and before that, the townsfolk were made to use the ford which crossed beside the bridge. On meeting a mini roundabout, cross the road, the A3100, to arrive back at the Library which was our starting point.

You can now reward yourself by choosing one of Godalming's many excellent pubs to enjoy a well earned drink. Cheers!

ACCOMMODATION

The Kings Arms and Royal Hotel, Godalming. Tel: 0483 421545
Virtually on the walk, this is a large historic hotel which has seen some distinguished guests.

The Parrot Inn, Shalford. Tel: 0483 61400
On the walk, accommodation is in a popular riverside pub. The rooms are comfortable and in the evening you do not have to go further than the pub restaurant for a good meal.

Youth Hostel, Hindhead YHA, Hindhead. Tel: 042860 4285
Approximately eight miles from the walk, this is a simple youth hostel situated in the bowl of the Devil's Punch Bowl. Basic but idyllic and I loved it. Camping is also permitted amongst the rabbits!

Camping and Caravanning, Whipley Manor Farm, Bramley. Tel: 0483 272816
One mile from the walk, this is a beautiful site situated on a large arable farm. Facilities are basic, but then that is the beauty of the site. Caravans are only allowed as members of the Caravan Club, but the campsite has no such restrictions.

THE WINTERFOLD WANDER

Distance: 10¼ miles (16.5 km)
Time: Allow approximately 5½ hours
Map: Ordnance Survey Landranger Maps 186 and 187

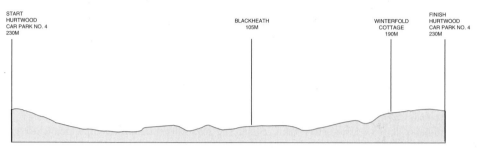

START
HURTWOOD
CAR PARK NO. 4
230M

BLACKHEATH
105M

WINTERFOLD
COTTAGE
190M

FINISH
HURTWOOD
CAR PARK NO. 4
230M

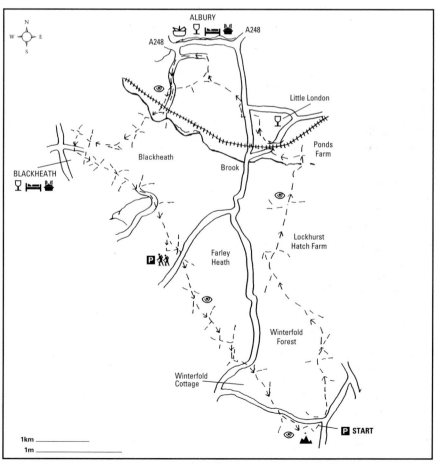

Walk Summary

This is a wonderful walk through some of the best heath and woodland in Surrey. Much of the scenery has remained unchanged since the days when smugglers trod the paths, some of which probably only came into being as a result of their dubious activities! Today, you are unlikely to spot a smuggler but keep your eyes peeled, as you will hopefully be rewarded by way of an insight into the wealth of wildlife which takes advantage of the vast cover the woods and heathland offer. Although this feels a remote walk, you are never far from a hamlet or village and three of Surrey's best pubs welcome you en route. This paradise does not however, come without effort, as some of the paths can be very muddy and the last third of the walk is mostly uphill (nothing extensive) along sandy tracks, which can severely test those calf muscles. Don't therefore, get too over enthusiastic with the local brew or the sand may bury you!

Start - OS. 075426 Map 187

The walk starts from Hurtwood car park, number four, which is at Raynards Hill at the southern edge of Winterfold Forest. To get there, by car, from the north it is best to make your way along the A25 to Shere and from there, take the road which leads south out of the village, signposted to Ewehurst and Cranleigh. Follow the road for approximately three miles and then take a narrow road right signposted to Winterfold. After a short distance, you will meet another road on the right which you should take to then turn immediately left into Hurtwood car park, number four. If coming from the south, make your way to Ewehurst on the B2127 and from there, take a road opposite "The Bull's Head", signposted to Peaslake, Shere and Gomshall. Follow the road past "The Windmill Inn" to shortly after, take a turning left signposted to Winterfold. Follow this for a short distance until you reach a turning right. Take this to turn immediately left into car park number four at Hurtwood.

The nearest railway station is at Chilworth and from there it is approximately a mile walk along a lane to join our route at Blackheath. An alternative start can be made from Blackheath where there is a small car park (OS. 036461 Map 186) or from Hurtwood car park, number eight, (OS. 051447 Map 187).

THE WINTERFOLD WANDER

P

Before we start our adventure, I believe it is worth learning a little of the history of the extensive woodland which we are about to explore and of the people who protect it.

i

Hurtwood. *The car park from where we start is managed by the Hurtwood Control Committee. The committee was set up to preserve the rights of the public after Reginald Bray of Shere generously donated Hurtwood to the public in 1926. The committee relied mainly upon the generosity of the local inhabitants to manage the wood, until it was re-organised in 1979 to allow funding to be obtained from public bodies and local authorities. The committee still manages the wood today and you will see more of their signs as the walk progresses. Incidentally, the "hurt" in Hurtwood is the old name for bilberries which still grow in abundance in the wood today.*

Leave the car park via the main entrance and cross a lane to take a signposted public bridleway the other side, ignoring another bridleway forking off to the left. The bridleway leads gently downhill through the beautiful sandstone woodland of Winterfold Forest and you should follow it, ignoring all turnings off, to eventually reach and pass through a wooden gate and join a track which continues ahead in the same direction.

After a short distance, the track you are following joins a more prominent track which continues ahead. Keep to the track ignoring all minor turnings off and crossing tracks, including a marked footpath, until you eventually meet a wide gravel crossing track. Cross this and follow a less prominent track ahead to, after approximately forty metres, meet another crossing track marked as a public bridleway.

Turn left along the crossing track which runs gently downhill, narrowing as it goes. You will again pass through some beautiful deciduous woodland and later pass a minature pond (more a large puddle), known as Dewdney's Well, which is in fact in the middle of the track. When I last walked this way there were three woodpeckers, two great spotted and one green woodpecker, all bathing in the pond. This is a very rare sight, seeing a woodpecker at all is a thrill and seeing three together really made my day. After approximately half a mile another bridleway joins from the right, which you should ignore to continue ahead now walking between banks.

Continue to follow the bridleway which leads downhill and eventually ends at a "T" junction, beside a garden belonging to a beautiful sandstone cottage on your left **(OS. 065446 Map 187)**. Turn right at the "T" junction along a track and follow it for approximately one hundred metres, (part of the route for "The Holmbury Hurt" from "10 Adventurous Walks in Surrey"), after which you should take a marked bridleway which forks right. This is in the form of a narrow path and runs behind a cottage on your left to soon lead out to a narrow tarmac lane. There is another signposted bridleway right here along a concrete drive, also signposted to "Lockhurst Hatch Farm", which you should ignore **(OS. 065449 Map 187)**.

Continue ahead along the lane (do not turn left), known as Ponds Lane and follow this between fields to sometime later pass a cottage on your left, the old well for which still sits in an adjacent field. After the cottage the lane goes over a rise and then bends right to lead into "Dilton Farm". You should leave the lane before it enters the farm and continue straight on along a signposted bridleway, which takes the form of a prominent path running gently downhill. After a short distance, ignore a marked footpath and stile off to the left and at the same time, take note of the view in the same direction which includes the prominent St. Martha's Hill with its famous church at the summit. Sometime later, ignore another footpath off to your right and continue, at one point passing a small abandoned coppice, to eventually reach the outbuildings of "Ponds Farm".

After passing a set of stone mounting steps on your left, go over a stile on the same side to join a tarmac path which runs between a fence on your left and a stone wall on the right. This soon leads to another stile which you should cross, beside the entrance to "Ponds House Farm", to continue ahead thereafter along the farm's tarmac drive. Follow the drive to later pass "Ponds Cottages" on your left, soon after which you will meet a lane. As a guide, the first houses of the hamlet of Brook are now on your left and a bridge, part of the railway line from Guildford to Redhill, is on your right.

The Redhill to Guildford Branch Line. *If you study the map you will notice that the railway line, for no apparent reason, takes a large curved detour south around Shere and Albury, instead of following the Tillingbourne which would be a much easier route. The reason for the detour which was made at great expense and involved skillful engineering, was one Henry Drummond. Drummond was once the owner of Albury Park and Lord of the Manor during the mid-19th century. The original plan was to run the railway in a straight line through Albury Park.*

Drummond was horrified at the prospect of having the view from his house ruined and refused to allow the engineers anywhere near Albury.

Despite the huge power of the railway companies, they were forced to abandon their plans and take the line around the park and Albury village, before returning to the original route at Chilworth. Their defeat demonstrates the huge power and influence that Henry Drummond commanded and although his reason was purely selfish, you must thank him for preserving a unique part of Surrey. I wonder if he would have had the same success against the Department of Transport today - I very much doubt it!

Turn right along the lane, pass under the railway bridge and at the other side take a signposted public footpath left in front of a sign for Little London, a small hamlet of Victorian origin. *If however, you are in need of refreshments, then it is worth taking a short detour by continuing along the lane to reach the "William IV" pub, a free house, at Little London. The pub is, in my opinion, one of the best in Surrey. Inside, it has changed little since smugglers of the heath used to drink here. Wooden benches sit on a flagstone floor, warmed in winter by a huge open fire. Also in winter, the pub has a small but excellent restaurant. Steak sandwiches can be ordered at the bar, a real saviour in cold weather. The one danger of stopping here is that you will never want to leave. With this warning, I would remind you that you need to retrace your steps to rejoin our route.*

The footpath at first, follows the line of the railway for a short distance before bending sharp right to go uphill. After passing between some metal railings, you will arrive at a drive to a cottage on your left. Bear right here and follow the drive to shortly after pass a brick storehouse on your right, where you should ignore three turnings off and continue ahead. The drive takes you across Albury Heath where, sometime later, you will meet a gravel crossing track. Go straight over the crossing track and join a signposted footpath the other side.

The footpath immediately forks and you should take the right hand fork which meanders across the heath and soon meets a junction of paths. Here, you should continue ahead along the main path which now runs gently uphill to cross a level hill top. At the hill top you will meet a junction of tracks beside a bench where I recommend you take a short breather. There are lovely views right to the cottages of Little London and beyond to Holmbury and the Hurtwood.

Our route from the junction of tracks is left, passing to the left of the bench. After a few paces, go over a crossing path to carry straight on (this can also be interpreted as taking the right hand fork, the more prominent path, continuing in the same direction). The path soon leads out to a lane which you should cross to follow a track ahead. After a few paces, turn right and pass between some wooden posts to follow the right hand perimeter of a cricket pitch. *You will soon pass a couple of wooden seats, in between which is a stone memorial errected here to commemorate Field Marshall Montgomery, popularly known as "Monty", who addressed the Canadian troops here in May 1944, before the D-Day landings. A maple tree has been planted either side of the memorial to commemorate the Canadian troops who lost their lives at the landing.*

The memorial is fairly recent. Montgomery's address had been kept so secret that the memorial was the first that many of Albury's life-long residents had heard of it. Whilst I was studying it, I met an eldery couple who were complaining bitterly about the damage badgers were doing to their cricket pitch. After exchanging pleasantries they continued on their way trying to find where these innocent vandals were making their entrance. They completely ignored a group of young children who were enjoying a game of football on the cricket pitch itself!

Continue to follow the perimeter of the cricket pitch to arrive at a parking area the other side and walk through the car park to meet a narrow tarmac lane which leads to the cricket clubhouse. Turn right along the lane for a few paces and take a signposted public bridleway on your left, just before a cottage. The bridleway, a narrow path, runs through a wooded area known as Albury Warren and after a short distance, goes straight over a crossing track to continue ahead. Soon after, you should ignore another path joining from the left and maintain your route ahead.

Sometime later, ignore a further crossing track and carry straight on where, to your left you can just make out a large house through the trees, which is in fact Albury Warren School. Go straight across an open grass clearing to arrive at a track in front of a pair of gates. Pass through the bridleway gate and continue ahead along the track the other side, in the direction of a blue bridleway arrow.

Stay on the track until you eventually see a signposted bridleway which leads off to the right, going downhill between banks **(OS. 054473 Map 187)**. Here you have a choice. Turning right (the official route), takes you through the village of Albury where you can enjoy some refreshment at "The Drummond Arms". Alternatively, if you have no wish to visit Albury, simply carry straight on, ignoring all turnings off, until you reach a lane. A distance of approximately one third of a mile **(OS. 049472 Map 186)**. Here you should rejoin the official route by going over a stile opposite into a field.

To follow the official route, as mentioned, turn right leaving the main track and follow the bridleway downhill along what is obviously an ancient route, known as Water Lane, probably because it once led to a water source at Albury Warren. Ignore a marked footpath off to the left sometime later where just after, the bridleway leaves Albury Warren to continue between fields. As it does so, look out for gates either side of the bridleway, which offer excellent view points across the North Downs. The left hand gate in particular, offers a view across to two churches, the church at Albury and beyond, St. Martha's church at the top of St. Martha's Hill.

Stay on the bridleway, still descending and pass between some sandstone cliffs with a number of magnificent beech and oak trees clinging precariously to their sides, with many of their tangled roots exposed. Soon after the cliffs, the bridleway bends left and you should ignore a track off to the right and a stile immediately after. The bridleway soon leads to a lane where you must ignore a footpath which descends steps on the right. Follow the lane ahead past the first houses of Albury to soon reach the village's unusual brick church.

Albury Parish Church (OS. 051477 Map 187) *is one of three churches in Albury, the other two being at Albury Park, the original site of the village. The church was built in 1842 by Henry Drummond to replace the derelict Saxon church in Albury Park. It was meant to be a copy of a church at Thaon in Normandy, France, though there is one glaring difference. The church at Thaon was built of stone.*

Stay on the lane passing Albury Bowling Club on the right, until it bends sharp right in front of an unusual hexagonal brick cottage. Our route leaves the lane at this point to join a narrow lane on the left, marked as Blackheath Lane. First however, I suggest you continue to follow the original lane to shortly reach the A248 and the heart of Albury village as well as "The Drummond Arms". You will have to retrace your steps to rejoin our route.

Albury (OS. 050478 Map 186) *is relatively modern, having been virtually rebuilt at the beginning of the 19th century, after the Lord of the Manor had forcibly evicted the villagers from the site of their original village, now Albury Park. Things looked pretty grim for the villagers until the energetic Henry Drummond purchased the estate in 1819 and threw himself wholeheartedly into the affairs of village life with varied results.*

To modernise the manor house and rebuild the village, Drummond employed the architect, Pugin, better known for his magnificent stone work at the Houses of Parliament. Pugin had a fascination for chimneys which allowed him to experiment without restriction, his love for ornate design. The chimneys at the eastern end of the village are a perfect example of this, where their impact and size are quite startling, bearing no relation to the size of the houses on which they sit.

Despite Drummond's efforts to revitalise the village, Albury was the scene in 1830, of one of the so-called Corn Riots. The Corn Riots were a consequence of farm mechanisation which allowed landowners to sack their manual labourers, many of whom were beginning to show dissent after years of suffering low wages whilst the old Corn Laws had kept food prices high. In 1830, the tensions which had been gradually mounting finally surfaced and farm labourers across the south united in revolt under the dubious leadership of one Captain Swing. In Albury, the farm labourers' anger was vented on the local corn mill which was burned to the ground with the owner being shot at as he tried to prevent the attack. One James Warner was arrested as a result and became the last man to be hanged for arson in England.

Albury's corn mill was one of many mills along the Tillingbourne valley, the others were mainly involved in the much more controversial manufacture of gunpowder and banknotes, which apart from wealth brought a fair amount of misery to the community. During the Great War the valley's gunpowder manufacture brought unwanted attention from the German airforce, which used a zepplin to drop bombs on the mills. Happily, when this happened no-one was killed. Today, the only disruption to the village is the A248 which runs through its centre, though by modern standards this is a minor inconvenience.

The village pub, "The Drummond Arms" remembers the new village's founder. The pub used to be a brewery and keeps up tradition by serving some good ales. Although quite plush, it retains a very relaxed atmosphere where you can enjoy a good value meal. Outside, the pub has a lovely garden backing on to the Tillingbourne. Just to the west of the pub opposite the village Post Office and general stores, sits a small triangular green with an ornate wooden signpost (this is where you enter Albury from the walk). Before the signpost, stood the village maypole which was apparently in use right up until the mid-19th century.

Antique fairs are held regularly at weekends in the Village Hall and a short visit may reward you with an unusual souvenir of your adventure, though first make sure it will fit in your rucksack!

Returning to our route, follow Blackheath Lane gently uphill between banks passing "Birmingham Farm" on your left. As you progress, the banks graduate into sandstone cliffs, soon after which you will pass a barn on the right. The lane then begins to descend at which point you should look out for a bridleway on the left and another on the right (**OS. 049472 Map 186**). (If you have bypassed Albury you will arrive from the bridleway on the left).

Take the bridleway on your right by going over a stile into a field. Turn immediately left and follow the left hand perimeter of the field where there are lovely views ahead to the wooded Blackheath. At the far side of the field, go over a stile and continue in the same direction across the next field. At the field end, pass through a kissing gate and go down a bank to cross a railway line. Pass through another kissing gate the other side and bear gently diagonally right across the centre of a field, heading for a stile at the far side. Go over the stile onto a farm track and turn right along the track, now going downhill, to shortly cross over a stream.

Follow the track up the other side of the valley after the stream, to soon meet some outbuildings belonging to "Postford Farm". After the outbuildings, take a signposted footpath left just in front of some attractive farm cottages. The footpath runs through a pretty strip of woodland which acts as a divider between fields, at the end of which it enters the wood of Blackheath. Here, you are immediately presented with a wide choice of routes with several paths fanning out in front of you. Take the second path from the right which leads uphill and at the top of the hill follow it as it bends left to meander through a beautiful area of pine, heathers and mosses.

The footpath eventually comes out at a sandy clearing where you should carry straight on, along the left hand side of the clearing, to shortly meet a sandy crossing track, marked by a blue topped post. Just before meeting this crossing track, you should ignore another track which joins from the left. Turn right, along the crossing track (as a guide this is a turning immediately right and is also the narrowest of all the routes here), and after a few paces, pass through some wooden rails and continue ahead through an area of open heather. The heather here in late summer/early autumn is a thick carpet of mauves and purples, with the air filled with the humming of eager bees. After a short distance, go over another crossing track,

The War Memorial on Blackheath

passing through two sets of wooden rails, to maintain your route ahead.

Sometime on, pass through another set of wooden rails to arrive at a large junction of tracks. Turn right here and follow a track, marked by a blue topped post and "P1", and follow this through the wood to soon meet a lane. Cross the lane and join a path the other side which immediately forks. Take the left hand fork which continues ahead, running in a straight line, and soon after, pass through some more wooden rails to leave the wood and arrive at a large clearing of heather and a stone war memorial on your right. Standing behind the war memorial, you can enjoy another excellent view across to St. Martha's church. The war memorial was built in memory of men from the village of Blackheath who died in the first World War.

Turn left and follow a narrow path along the perimter of the wood with the heather clearing on your right. The path soon crosses a small stretch of the clearing and on reaching the tree line the other side, bends sharp right to continue along the perimeter of the clearing. After a short distance, the path bends sharp left to once more wind through woodland, predominantly made up of silver birch and firs. It soon leads to a car park for "The Villagers" pub, Pheonix breweries, at Blackheath.

The pub is quite unexpected and a pleasant surprise. Inside is a huge spacious bar where apart from beer, you can stock up with the pub's wholesome food. The pub also offers bed and breakfast and is an excellent place to stay if you are looking to get away from it all. The village itself, like Albury, stems from the 19th century, though there was no previous village and no selfish Lord of the Manor here. Blackheath instead, is the creation of travellers who decided to set up permanent homes here. Before them, the only previous permanent occupants of the heath were the Romans.

On reaching the road in front of the pub, cross this and join a fenced path the other side, which runs between gardens and shortly meets a track. Turn left along the track to arrive at Blackheath cricket field, where in summer you have another opportunity to rest and enjoy a game. Stay on the track, passing to the left of the cricket field and to the right some houses with balconies, which afford the owners an advantageous view of the cricket. Note also the nets which protect the windows, Blackheath obviously has some hard hitters. Perhaps someone should mention this to the England selectors!

At the far side of the cricket field the track bends sharp left and you should leave it here to join a narrow path ahead, which soon meets a prominent crossing path. You should ignore this and continue ahead to shortly meet and cross a second crossing path and follow a more prominent footpath ahead, marked by a blue topped post and "303". You should follow the "303" footpath all the way through the wood until you eventually meet a lane (**OS. 044457 Map 186**). The following description therefore, is given merely as a guide and in case some of the markers are missing.

The footpath winds through the familiar and beautiful woodland of Blackheath. You should ignore all turnings off until you eventually meet a wide crossing track, which you should cross to maintain your route ahead, still following the path marked "303". After a few paces, ignore another path joining from the left and carry straight on, keeping to the main path at all times and ignoring any further turnings off or crossing paths. The footpath eventually leads out to a lane beside a weather boarded bungalow on the right (**OS. 044457 Map 186**). As a guide, on your left here is a Waverley District Council Countryside map of Blackheath.

Join the lane to carry straight on, at one point passing a lovely white house and when the lane bends sharp right, leave it to take a signposted bridleway left. The bridleway takes the form of a sandy track and after approximately twenty metres, it bends left. You should leave it here and join a narrow path on the right, which runs between banks going gently uphill. The banks close in and become steeper as you progress, so much so that at one point you almost rub shoulders with the banks either side. The path is so deep that your head at times is below the level of the ground. It is a perfect smugglers route and one wonders what sort of contraband has passed this way over the years.

Eventually, the banks either side give way and you will meet a junction of tracks. Here you should ignore two tracks, more like paths, off to the left and right respectively and continue ahead along a wide sandy track, thereby maintaining your route. Soon after, look out for a marked bridleway on the left opposite a gate on your right, which you should take to shortly arrive at a grass clearing used as a car park, Hurtwood car park number eight.

Turn right and follow the right hand perimeter of the car park, ignoring a bridleway off to the right. On reaching a lane, cross this and join a signposted public bridleway the other side (ignore a track forking left), which takes the form of a sandy track and runs in an almost straight line across more wooded heathland, Farley Heath.

The Romans at Farley Heath. *Today, Farley Heath connects Blackheath with Winterfold Forest and is one of the remotest areas in Surrey. Things were very different in Roman times, when a road left Stane Street to cross the heath taking Roman soldiers from the south coast to the Midlands. The road, unlike many others, is no longer visible though it is known that it was still in use during the reign of King John. Not far from where we stand a Roman station or camp, was discovered complete with a Romano British temple. The camp was quite large and probably supported a whole legion which would have consisted of around six thousand men. The site was always known over the centuries as Old Bury, which more recently has been corrupted to "Albury". Further south, near the same road, a Roman brick kiln was discovered suggesting that it was the Romans who brought brick making to the Weald, an industry which still thrives in the area today.*

After a short distance, the track narrows to become a wide path and runs gently uphill to later meet a prominent crossing track, which you should ignore to continue ahead still going gently uphill. On meeting a second crossing track, go over this and carry straight on to soon meet a fork. Take the left hand fork, thereby leaving the bridleway, to join a sandy track which is unmarked. The sand and gradual climb certainly test your fitness and if you have spent too long at "The Villagers", you are probably about now beginning to regret it!

Sometime on, you will meet a junction of tracks where you should ignore a track coming in from the left, to take the second turning left, a narrow path. This follows the line of some fields on your left and affords excellent views in the same direction to the North Downs, where on a clear day the spire of Ranmore church is visible. After a short distance the path bends right to arrive at a "T" junction, where you should turn left to follow a wider path, thereby rejoining the original track, now going downhill.

Ignore a marked footpath off to your left soon after joining and continue ahead to follow the track downhill, ignoring any further turnings off and then very gently uphill until you reach a fork. Take the left hand fork, the more prominent path and ignore as you join it a grass path off to your left. Shortly after, ignore two further grass paths off to your left just before meeting a crossing path. Turn left along the crossing path which now runs uphill, to soon arrive at a "T" junction in the form of a sunken track. This is another ancient track known as Ride Lane.

Turn right along the track, admiring the ancient moss covered banks topped by regal beech trees as you progress. After approximately two hundred metres, the track forks where you should keep to the main track, that is the left hand fork. After the fork the track bends left and you should ignore any turnings off to the left or right, including a marked footpath on the left. Continue to shortly go over another crossing track and maintain your route ahead for a few paces along a narrow path, to meet a lane (**OS. 062433 Map 187**). Cross the lane and join a signposted bridleway the other side, also signposted to "Winterfold Cottage", a clue that you are now back in Winterfold Forest and not too far from our starting point.

Follow the bridleway ignoring any turnings off, until you meet the entrance to the cottage and here, take a path which runs to the left of the cottage and goes gently downhill, following the garden perimeter. As you progress, ignore another path which joins from the left and carry straight on and a few paces further on, ignore a marked public footpath also off to the left. The path you are following soon bends gently left away from the cottage and its garden, to commence the home stretch through Winterfold Forest. Like so many other paths on this walk, the path is soon bordered by banks.

Sometime on, a path joins from the right and just after, you will meet a wide crossing track beside a gate on your left. Go over the crossing track and join a path the other side which bears diagonally right, away from the gate mentioned and follow this in a straight line through beautiful silver birch woodland. The path follows the course of the Roman road which guided Roman soldiers across the heath. Today, there can be no harder picture to imagine than a line of colourful Roman soldiers marching towards you.

Sometime later, a marked bridleway joins from the left and as before, you should ignore this to maintain your route ahead to eventually arrive at a lane. Cross the lane and turn left to follow it for a few paces to meet a junction of three tracks. Take the left hand track to go straight on, marked by a yellow arrow and "GW", the latter indicating that you are now joining the Greensand Way. This runs parallel with the lane on your left.

Sometime later, you will meet a crossing path which you should go over and carry straight on. Shortly after, the path bends right to bear away from the lane and meanders across the wooded top of Raynards Hill to later meet a "T" junction. Turn left, in the direction of a yellow arrow and the "GW" marker and continue ignoring any turnings off along the edge of Raynards Hill. You will soon meet a raised view point and a bench, known as Lord Justice James Seat, where you can enjoy stunning views across the Surrey Weald and the South Downs. The views are a fitting finale to the walk and all the more enjoyable with the knowledge that our starting point is only two minutes walk away (and downhill!). To get there, return to the path which bends left away from the edge of the hill and view point and follow it gently downhill to shortly arrive back at Hurtwood car park, number four, and our starting point.

ACCOMMODATION

The Drummond Arms, Albury. Tel: 048641 2039
Virtually on the walk, this is a wonderful place to stay allowing you to explore the
Tillingbourne valley at your leisure. The accommodation, like the rest of the pub, is
quite smart but relaxed and very comfortable.

The Villagers, Blackheath. Tel: 0483 893152
On the walk, this pub is a must if you want to get away from it all. Accommodation
is in four chalet style bedrooms, each with its own garden. Special weekend walking
breaks are on offer.

Youth Hostel, Holmbury YHA, Holmbury St. Mary. Tel: 0306 730777
Approximately four miles from the walk, this is a purpose built youth hostel set in
large attractive grounds. The youth hostel can be busy in summer with school
parties - so be warned. Camping is permitted in the grounds.

Camping, Polesden Lacey, Dorking. Tel: 0372 456844
Approximately ten miles from the walk, this is a Camping and Caravanning Club
site in a beautiful setting on an old cricket pitch in the grounds of Polesden Lacey
House, N.T. Please note, that only tents and trailer tents are permitted.

IN PILGRIMS' FOOTSTEPS

Distance: 10½ miles (17 km)
Time: Allow approximately 5 hours
Map: Ordnance Survey Landranger Map 187

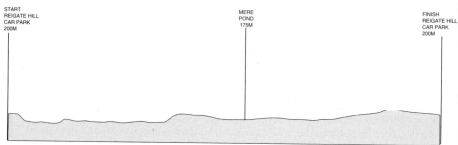

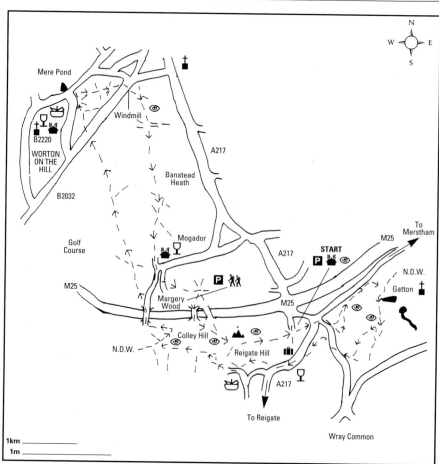

58

Walk Summary

In Pilgrims' Footsteps explores the sharply rising downs above Reigate and the heathland behind them which intrudes into the suburbs of London. On the way you will discover some surprising curiosities and if you keep your eyes peeled, a fair amount of wildlife. The going is fairly easy except for one extremely steep ascent of Colley Hill. Your efforts however, are rewarded by some excellent views across the Weald to the South Downs. One word of warning, at one point you will cross the A217 which can be extremely busy and children and animals should be kept under close control.

Start - OS. 263524 Map 187

The walk starts from the car park at the top of Reigate Hill. The car park is easily reached as it is off the A217, just south of junction 8 of the M25. If you are coming from Reigate there is no right turn into the car park and you will have to continue to the junction with the M25, doing a complete circle at the roundabout to return on the southern flow of the A217. The car park is reached by taking the first turning on the left after the roundabout, signposted to Merstham. Immediately upon joining, turn right and follow the car park signs to turn right again shortly after into the car park. As the book goes to print, the council is planning to upgrade the car parking facilities on Reigate Hill, so the entrance to the car park may change. Look out for the signs.

If coming by train, the nearest railway station is at Reigate which sits on the eastern side of the A217. It is about a mile walk, albeit uphill, to reach the car park.

An alternative start can be made from the National Trust car park at Margery Wood (OS. 245527).

IN PILGRIMS' FOOTSTEPS

Starting from the car park at Reigate Hill you are rewarded without effort with magnificent views over Reigate and the Surrey Weald to the South Downs. The only thing that spoils all this is the car park itself which with its run down lavatories and refreshment kiosk (which incidentally serves excellent tea), has become a favourite stop-over for motorway traffic, resulting in the car park becoming little more than a rubbish tip. The council, recognising the problem, are now planning to upgrade the car park by restricting access to larger vehicles and building an information and visitors centre, similar to the National Trust complex at Box Hill. Let's hope when you do this walk, that the centre has become a reality.

From the car park stand with your back to the kiosk facing the views across the Weald and turn left to shortly meet a lane, Wray Lane. Cross the lane and continue ahead along a wide track into Gatton Park, marked by a National Trust sign, also following the directions of the North Downs Way, easily recognised by the white acorns on a black background. The track soon bends right and also begins to descend, just after which you should ignore another track off to the left. Soon after, the track forks and here you should take the left hand fork, thereby keeping to the more prominent track and still following the North Downs Way.

On meeting a second fork approximately twenty metres on, take the right hand track thereby leaving the North Downs Way and after approximately ten metres, bear left to go over a stile and arrive at open grass hillside. Bear gently left following a narrow path diagonally down the side of the hill to shortly reach a wooden seat. Here you can enjoy excellent views across Gatton Park to the North Downs above Merstham.

From the seat, turn left to pass in front of it and then bear gently right to slowly continue descending the hillside until you reach a more prominent path running along the side of the hill. Turn left along the path and ignore a stile beside a bench on your left. Immediately after, you should also ignore a higher path and keep to the lower one which runs along the hillside, to shortly meet a stile. Go over the stile and continue ahead along a narrow path which runs through woodland made up mainly of hawthorne and sycamore. Ignore all minor turnings off staying on the path until it meets a track, where you should turn right thereby rejoining the North Downs Way.

After approximately twenty paces you will meet another track which joins from the left. You should ignore this to continue ahead with the very noisy M25 on your left running parallel with your route for a short while. The track eventually leads out to a tarmac drive beside a cottage on your left. Turn right along the drive which is signposted as a bridleway and still part of the North Downs Way and after a short distance, pass through a metal gate to enter the grounds of Gatton Park School and continue ahead along the drive.

Just after the drive bends left and at the end of an adventure playground on your right, turn right thereby leaving the North Downs Way for a second time, to almost go back on yourself passing a small private car park, which has room for about four cars, on the left. Before continuing however, you may wish to divert a little by following the drive (the North Downs Way) for a short distance, to visit Gatton church which sits beside a mansion, "Gatton Hall".

i
†
■

Gatton (OS. 275529 Map 187) *is most well known for once having been the third most "rotten borough" in the country. A rotten borough was a borough which sent members to Parliament despite having a minimal or even no electorate. This part of Surrey revelled in rotten boroughs as both nearby Reigate and Bletchingly had similar reputations. Gatton though, was the most blatant, when in 1451 the owner was granted the privilege of sending two members to Parliament. As the owner of "Gatton Hall" was generally the only resident of Gatton, his voting power in being able to select two MP's was considerable! The traveller and writer, Cobbett, a staunch supporter of fair play and rights for the common man, declared Gatton, "a very rascally spot of earth".*

Owning Gatton of course, brought considerable power and in 1830, Lord Monson purchased the borough and the voting rights that went with it, for one hundred thousand pounds. This was a considerable sum in those days and demonstrates the power and benefits that a rotten borough brought its owner. Unfortunately for Lord Monson, the same year in which he purchased the estate a general election was held after the death of George IV and the Whigs under Lord Grey came to power on a promise of electorial reform and the end of the corrupt rotten boroughs. Two years later in 1832, the reform bill was passed and the power of the rotten boroughs was passed to the large towns that had no representatives in Parliament. Gatton borough hence, became Gatton Park and a very expensive one at that! Lord Monson however, to his credit, put his bad investment behind him and set about building "Gatton Hall", which he boasted would be the most superb in the land. Unfortunately, the house burned down in 1934 and his efforts have been lost. A new imposing house was built, but from all accounts is no replacement for the original.

The church which you can visit, dates from the 13th century and inside is filled with artefacts brought back by Lord Monson from all over Europe. Monson appears to have had a love affair with wood, which dominates the church. The magnificent wooden baroque stalls are from Ghent, the panelling was taken from cathedrals in Brabant and Burgundy and the alter rails from Tongres in Belgium. The pulpit and alter both come from Nuremberg. There is much more to see, making the church a sort of museum of religious architecture.

Close to the church is a minature copy of a greek temple with a large urn. Built in 1765, this was Gatton's "town hall", where a mock election would be held to send members to Parliament. On the urn an inscription in latin reads,

"When the lots have been drawn, the urn remains,
Let the well-being of the people be the supreme law,
The place of the assembly of Gatton 1765,
Let evil deception be absent".

Was the writer serious or was it a joke? Then, amazingly, it was probably meant to be serious.

A later owner of Gatton Park was Sir Jeremiah Coleman, famous for his mustard. Sir Jeremiah in fact often joked that he had become rich from something that most people left on the side of their plate! In 1952, he dontated over one hundred acres of the park to the National Trust. When he left the hall a trust was set up and Gatton Park became the Royal Alexandra and Albert School. More recently, the park has been sliced in half by the M25, though even this has failed to destroy its peaceful composure.

Returning to our route, after the car park continue ahead along a track and follow it, ignoring a minor path which leads downhill to some small lakes just visible on your left (private). The lakes were once hammer ponds. After passing through a gate, stay on the track as it bends left to soon run between fields. There are clear views left here of the North Downs escarpment and right to the hill we were on earlier. Behind to your left as you continue, the magnificent frontage of "Gatton Hall" is also just visible.

Eventually, the fields either side of the track end and just after this you will arrive at a fork where you should take the right hand fork, thereby leaving the main track, to pass through a one bar wooden gate. Approximately ten paces after, take a track right which leads steeply uphill and almost back on yourself and, soon after joining, ignore a path off to the left to carry straight on. The track continues to climb and bends gently left to later pass a seat on your right, a good place for a rest and also another view point over the lakes of Gatton Park, Merstham and beyond, the North Downs.

Follow the track to soon pass a chestnut coppice on your right with more mature woodland on the left. Once again, you should ignore all minor turnings off to eventually arrive at a clearing where there is another seat. Carry straight on here, going over a crossing track and join a narrow path further ahead. This soon leads gently downhill and later passes over a crossing track to continue descending and shortly after meets a wooden fence. You should follow the path and the wooden fence ahead, to pass through a set of wooden rails, after which you should turn left to follow a brick wall down to Wray Lane.

Cross the lane and join a signposted bridleway the other side which is fenced and runs along the lower slopes of Reigate Hill. There are good views to your left in places here over the more affluent parts of Reigate and beyond to Leith Hill. The bridleway eventually leads out onto a tarmac drive where there is a house on your right. Bear left to follow the drive and when this ends in front of "Wray Lane House", continue ahead along a fenced grass path which runs between gardens. The gardens soon end and the path continues through the more natural woodland of Reigate Hill.

Stay on the path to eventually arrive at another tarmac drive, where again you should continue ahead to shortly arrive at the noisy A217. Turn left along the A217 to go downhill. This rude interruption to the walk is but a short one, as after approximately one hundred metres as the road bends left, you should cross it to join a signposted public bridleway the other side, also marked as a "No Through Road" (OS. 256517). Crossing here can be quite dangerous and it is probably better to continue for a few paces more and cross opposite a garage and "The Yew Tree" pub. The garage has a shop which sells basic refreshments should you wish to stock up, though probably much more preferable is "The Yew Tree", which despite being on a main road, still retains a good atmosphere, helped by its wooden panelled bar. The food is good value and real ale is served. You will have to continue up the A217 to reach the bridleway (OS. 256517).

The first ten metres of the bridleway is tarmacced and runs between cottages before arriving at a fork. You should leave the tarmac drive here to take a track on the left (left fork), which is fenced and runs along the lower slopes of Reigate Hill. As you progress, the fences either side of the track change to become brick walls and the bridleway passes to the left of a large house which is actually built into the side of the hill. After this, you will arrive at a tarmac drive leading to "Underbeeches", which you should cross, at the same time ignoring a path off to your right going uphill. Continue ahead to, after a few paces, arrive at a lane onto which you should turn right.

Follow the lane between yet more grand properties to soon arrive at a parking area in front of a gate and a National Trust sign for the Pilgrims Way.

i **The Pilgrims Way** *until recently was believed to have been a continuous track from Winchester to Canterbury. It is now apparent that this was almost certainly not the case and that the route was simply by way of very local paths and tracks. It has even been suggested that the pilgrimage from Winchester to Canterbury is no more than Victorian fantasy. I for one, if only for personal pleasure and the enjoyment of treading a path once used by pilgrims, prefer not to believe this.*

PILGRIMS WAY

The Pilgrims Way is reputed to have come into being after the murder of Thomas a Becket on the alter at Canterbury cathedral. Becket died in defence of his faith and the church against his one time friend, Henry II, who wished to be King of the church. Becket's murderers further attempted to demonstrate the King's power and contempt of the church by spreading his brain over the cathedral floor. Their ugly deed backfired and Thomas a Becket became Saint Thomas, his tomb in the cathedral becoming one of the most important shrines in Europe. As a result, in theory, the Pilgrims Way was born with pilgrims making their way from Winchester, our country's ancient capital, along one of the oldest routes in the land to Canterbury. Tradition has it that Henry II even started the pilgrimage, when as an act of repentance he walked the route barefoot in 1174, though this is now also hotly disputed by modern historians.

Much of the modern belief stems from the fact that the Pilgrims Way is marked as a long distance route on the ordnance survey map. The man responsible for this was Captain Edward James and it is now evident by his notes, that whilst surveying in Surrey he became fascinated with the story of the Pilgrims Way and promptly marked his own interpretation of the route on the map. Thus, almost overnight,  *unintentionally he created supposedly, the best evidence that the Pilgrims Way existed.*

On the Pilgrims Way

There is however, evidence on the ground that pilgrims did travel from Winchester to Canterbury. Along the way, there are several roads called "pilgrims" which pre-date Victorian fantasy and ordnance survey maps and several churches give hints to there once having been a pilgrimage. For example, churches dedicated to St. James, the patron saint of pilgrims, pre-dating the Victorian era, are dotted along the route. One of the most famous churches in Surrey, St. Martha's, uses the scallop shell as its emblem, a symbol from another famous and ancient centre of pilgrimage, Compostella in Spain.

Whatever the truth, what we do know is that this part of the Pilgrims Way really is an ancient track, frequently referred to as the "Old Road" and over the centuries used by our neolithic ancestors, Romans, Saxons and Danes, if not pilgrims.

Pass between a wooden rail to the left of the gate and continue ahead along the Pilgrims Way, which now runs along the bottom of the wooded slopes of Colley Hill. Sometime on, the path forks and you should take the left hand fork, which leads down the side of a bank and then over a crossing path before passing through some wooden rails to arrive at an open meadow. Carry straight on along the left hand perimeter of the meadow, following a fairly well defined grass path. This is a beautiful spot and a favourite place for people from Reigate to picnic. The meadow which in summer is a mass of chalk flowers is overlooked by the magnificent backdrop of Colley Hill and to your left affords lovely views across the Weald and to Leith Hill.

At the far side of the meadow, pass through a kissing gate beside a farm gate and a few paces on, turn right at a "T" junction to follow a narrow path heading towards Colley Hill. Shortly after, pass through a set of wooden rails to soon meet a prominent crossing path. Turn left onto the crossing path which follows the base of Colley Hill. You are now entering a wonderful world of English woodland, which in places can seem more like an equatorial rain forest, especially after a short summer shower during the steamy aftermath of the evapourating droplets.

Stay on the path as it skirts the bottom of the hill, ignoring all turnings off and note in places a number of large wooded craters, which are the remains of quarrying some years ago. At the steeper parts of the path, the National Trust have introduced steps to assist your progress, at the same time preventing unnecessary erosion. After walking through a small yew wood with lovely views left to Priory Hill, you will eventually pass through some wooden rails to meet a wide crossing path, where there is a sign for the North Downs Way.

Turn right onto the crossing path to go uphill in the direction of the North Downs Way sign. One word of warning here, take extra care at weekends, as this particular track is a favourite descent for groups of mountain bikers, often testing their speed and ability - the only thing you are likely to see are bright flashes of colour as they speed by! The path runs between banks becoming steeper as you go and gradually bends left and later sharp left. You should leave it as it bends sharp left and go up a bank to join a narrow path ahead. As a guide, this is just before a post marked by the familiar white acorn of the North Downs Way **(OS. 242522).** Take care not to miss it.

The path continues to climb and runs along the side of the steep escarpment of Colley Hill, where in places when the trees allow, you will enjoy marvellous views right across the side of Colley Hill to Reigate Hill and beyond. As before, the National Trust have provided steps at the steeper points along the path to help you on your way. When the steps end, the path bends right and continues along the edge of the hill to soon arrive at open grass hillside, with excellent views across the Weald to the South Downs.

On reaching the open hillside, you should immediately turn left to follow a prominent path, almost going back on yourself. This leads through an area of scrub and after going over a "V" stile, it meets a wide track beside a National Trust sign for Colley Hill. Turn left along the track where you will once again hear the noise of the M25, and just before the track forks in front of some wooden rails and a North Downs Way marker, notice a white post marked by a shield and red cross on your right. These once marked the coal boundary around London, a toll had to be paid on all coal shipments which crossed the boundary into London.

Ignore a narrow path right here and continue ahead taking the right hand fork. The track soon bends right and continues to meet a lane beside another white coal post. Turn right along the lane to shortly cross the M25 and at the other side, take a signposted public bridleway on your left which runs parallel with the motorway for a short while. Soon after, it bends away from the motorway and runs through a pretty oak and silver birch wood. You should stay on the bridleway, carrying straight on and ignore any turnings off to the left or right. As you progress, the greens of Walton Heath Golf Course will come into view on your left. The golf course is famous locally for staging the Ryder Cup in 1981.

Sometime on, you will pass another white coal post where you should ignore a crossing path to continue ahead. Pass a third white post in the middle of the path to shortly after, meet a prominent crossing path in front of a fourth white post. Go over the crossing path and carry straight on, passing to the left of the white post and stay on the bridleway to eventually leave the wood and follow a hedged path across Banstead Heath, with the golf course on your left and open grassland on your right. The route continues to pass in places, the white coal posts, the bridleway therefore, now following the old coal boundary for London.

The bridleway eventually meets a junction of paths just before the start of another area of woodland. You should follow a gravel track ahead from here, marked as a bridleway, which runs to the left of the woodland and to the right of the golf course. As you progress, the track narrows to become more of a path and begins to descend. Continue ahead, ignoring all turnings off and keep to the perimeter of the woodland and the golf course on your left. At one point, a fairly prominent path joins your route from the right and you should ignore this to carry straight on. A few paces thereafter, the bridleway forks and you should take the left hand fork to continue ahead.

Shortly after, the bridleway forks again. As before, you should take the left hand fork and follow this to eventually arrive at a road, the B2032 **(OS. 230548)**. Cross the road and join a tarmac drive the other side, signposted to "Walton House" and immediately after joining, take a signposted public footpath right. A few paces on, the footpath forks and you should take the left hand fork, passing to the left of a byelaws sign for Banstead Common. Thereafter, pass through a set of wooden rails and follow the footpath ahead to soon pass to the right of a house.

The path now continues in a straight line ahead and, once again, you should ignore all turnings off to the left or right, to eventually arrive at "The Blue Ball" pub, which confusingly has a windmill as its sign. The windmill pictured stands nearby and is on our route. A blue ball was something held up to show the end of a horse race, the pub probably got its name because of its close proximity to Epsom race course. The pub itself which is Victorian, is a free house serving some respectable ales. The huge bar has been over-decorated for my tastes but still retains a good atmosphere. Apart from serving bar snacks there is a popular restaurant at the rear. Alternatively, you can simply enjoy a pint and bag of crisps outside overlooking the common.

Follow the path past the pub to arrive at a road, Walton Street, opposite a small pond and a general stores on your left. Do not cross the road, but turn right instead opposite the general stores and take a prominent gravel path, more a track, which leads almost back on yourself across the common.

The gravel track although unmarked is a bridleway and the gravel soon gives way to well hoofed earth. After a short distance, you will meet a tarmac crossing path which you should cross to carry straight on. Soon after, you should meet and cross another crossing path to maintain your route, keeping to the track which is still a bridleway. After the second crossing path, a variation of paths will cross your route from different directions. At all times, you should ignore these and continue straight on to eventually arrive at the main road, the B2032.

Cross the B2032 and join the bridleway the other side which runs through Banstead Heath woodland and follows the perimeter of a property on your left. The bridleway soon leads out to the open grassland of Banstead Heath and from here you will enjoy marvellous views ahead to your right of the northern side of the North Downs. The two aerial masts ahead to your right in the distance, are those at Reigate fort and slightly to the right of them, you can just discern the square top of the old water *i* tower at the top of Colley Hill. Immediately to your left behind a hedge stands the body of an old wooden windmill. Sadly, the sails are long gone. The windmill dates from the 18th century and last saw service in 1902.

On reaching the open grassland, ignore a wide grass crossing track and continue ahead to meet a second crossing track, approximately fifty metres on. Turn right onto the crossing track to now head south and commence our return journey to Reigate Hill. When the track forks, take the left hand fork and follow this downhill, ignoring any further crossing tracks or turnings off, to soon pass through a small copse and continue downhill to thereafter, follow the perimeter of a wood on your left. You will now descend to the bottom of a valley where you will meet a junction of paths. You should ignore all these and carry straight on along a wide track up the other side of the valley through a wood. Ignore all turnings off and continue ahead to later meet a fork.

Take the right hand fork and after a few paces, go straight over a wide crossing track and join a very narrow footpath the other side (slightly to your right). In summer this can be somewhat hidden in bracken and you may have to hunt it out. Follow the path through the bracken which in summer, can be very tall and offer its own adventure, the path becoming more prominent as you progress. You should ignore all minor turnings off and in summer, take advantage of the bracken and the natural camouflage that it offers, to pause as you walk and enjoy the wildlife around you.

Eventually, after much twisting and turning which can be quite exhausting when the bracken is at its height, you will arrive at a wide crossing track at the other side of the wood. Go over the track and pass through a gap in the hedge ahead to follow a narrow but fairly prominent path straight on. This leads down the side of a shallow valley to meet the edge of a strip of woodland, where you should take a prominent path through the wood to the other side. Once at the other side, bear right along a narrow path following the perimeter of the wood along the bottom of the valley. When the path later bends right through the wood once more, leave it to continue straight on and after approximately fifty paces, arrive at a junction of paths. Carry straight on here to now follow another strip of woodland, this time on your left **(OS. 240539).**

You will now climb gently uphill where, as you progress, it is worth stopping to look back at the view. In the distance on a clear day, you can just make out the windmill passed earlier. Continue to follow the perimeter of the wood on your left which gradually bends left, to eventually pass between some wooden posts beside a single white rail onto a tarmac lane. Carry straight on to shortly arrive at "The Sportsman" pub, Courage, which is in a beautiful location at the edge of Walton Heath.

i **The Sportsman (OS. 239532 Map 187)** *dates from the 16th century and was originally built as a Royal hunting lodge. Today, the best things to hunt are the real ales which often include the excellent Pilgrim Ale and wholesome home-made food. If you have been surprised at how deserted the heath appeared you will now realise why as it often seems, that all the walkers in Surrey are here! Often joining the company are horse riders who take advantage of the rail provided by the pub to tether their horses. If you have never been here before, the pub comes as an excellent discovery and I guarantee you will return.*

Facing the pub is a small green and dew pond. The pond which is man-made, as the name suggests, ingeniously collects dew for its water. A well built pond was in times of drought more reliable than a spring and was essential to farmers. This particular pond served the commoners who used the heath to graze their animals.

After "The Sportsman", follow the lane ahead and stay on it as it bends round to the left. Ignore a signposted bridleway off to the right and on reaching a "T" junction, turn right along another lane. Shortly after, join a signposted bridleway on your left, passing between some white topped posts to do so and continue to initially run parallel to the lane before meeting a "T" junction in the form of a prominent path, marked on the map as a bridleway. Turn left along the bridleway to shortly meet a lane which you should cross to join another bridleway the other side.

The bridleway traverses a shallow valley with a decaying orchard on your left and eventually arrives at another lane with a footpath off to the left and a National Trust parking area for Margery Wood on your right. Turn right and then right again into the car park and cross the car park to take a well trodden path at the far corner. This leads into the wood and you should stay on it, ignoring all turnings off, to cross the M25 once more, by way of a narrow footbridge. At the other side, follow the path ahead through woodland to soon meet a crossing track at the top of Colley Hill, also part of the North Downs Way. **P** **𝕩**

Turn left onto the crossing track where after a few paces, you will see a track on the left leading to a large brick water tower, the inscription at the front reading, "The Sutton District Water Company - 1911". Follow the track and the North Downs Way past the tower along the top of the hill, where there are gaps in the hedge on your right which lead out to open hillside. You can walk parallel to the track along the open hillside if you prefer, as long as you ensure you follow the hilltop and do not change direction. It is not long before the track also gives way to open hillside, where you are rewarded with the familiar views of the Weald and the line of the South Downs. Immediately below, you can also see the windmill at Reigate Heath and Reigate itself. Also visible is Leith Hill and the North Downs escarpment going westwards. This is a perfect place for a rest before the last mile to our finishing point. *i* *◎*

Continue along the North Downs Way along the top of the hill to shortly pass a stone temple-like structure.

The Colley Hill Fountain (OS. 249521 Map 187). *The temple was in fact built to* *i*

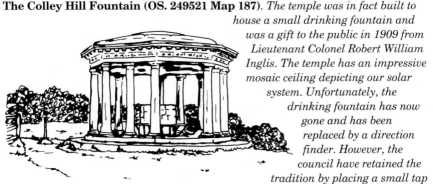

house a small drinking fountain and was a gift to the public in 1909 from Lieutenant Colonel Robert William Inglis. The temple has an impressive mosaic ceiling depicting our solar system. Unfortunately, the drinking fountain has now gone and has been replaced by a direction finder. However, the council have retained the tradition by placing a small tap beside the monument. Apart from helping people with their directions, the monument's most common purpose these days is sheltering walkers from inclement weather.

After the temple the track enters woodland at the top of Reigate Hill, much of it devastated in the infamous storm of 1987. The National Trust have been busy replanting, although successive dry summers since 1987, have slowed the progress of the rejuvenation. The track later passes the banks of Reigate Hill fort on the right.

i **Reigate Hill Fort (OS. 257522 Map 187)** *was built during the second World War as part of a defensive line along the North Downs protecting London in case of invasion. During the war the fort was manned by Canadian troops. Today, the only real use the fort enjoys is as an adventure campsite for cub scouts, though the council are now talking about making it into a tourist and education centre.*

After passing two aerial masts on your left, which act as a major landmark for Reigate Hill for miles around, the track soon meets a lane. Follow the lane ahead and as this bends left, leave it to carry straight on along another track, at the same time ignoring a signposted bridleway off to the right. Stay on the track to eventually cross the A217 via an old ornate iron bridge to arrive at the car park which was our starting point.

ACCOMMODATION

Cranleigh Hotel, Reigate. Tel: 0737 223417
One and a half miles from the walk, the Cranleigh Hotel is a smart friendly hotel, complete with attractive gardens and a heated open air swimming pool.

Reigate Manor Hotel, Reigate. Tel: 0737 240125
Virtually on the walk, this is quite a smart hotel converted from a Georgian mansion. The bedrooms are well furnished and should you feel like even more exercise, there is a fitness studio.

Youth Hostel, Tanners Hatch YHA, Polesden Lacey, Dorking. Tel: 0372 52528
Approximately eight miles from the walk, Tanners Hatch is an isolated cottage (you can only reach it by foot). Situated in the woods of Ranmore Common the hostel has no electricity, so bring your own lighting. Camping is also permitted.

Camping, Polesden Lacey, Dorking. Tel: 0372 456844
Five miles from the walk, this is a Camping and Caravanning Club site in a beautiful setting on an old cricket pitch in the grounds of Polesden Lacey, NT. Please note that only tents and trailer tents are permitted.

FRIDAY'S HURT

Distance: 12½ miles (20 km)
Time: Allow approximately 6½ hours
Map: Ordnance Survey Landranger Map 187

START	ABINGER	HOLMBURY HILL	FINISH
FRIDAY STREET	HAMMER	FORT	FRIDAY STREET
150M	90M	261M	150M

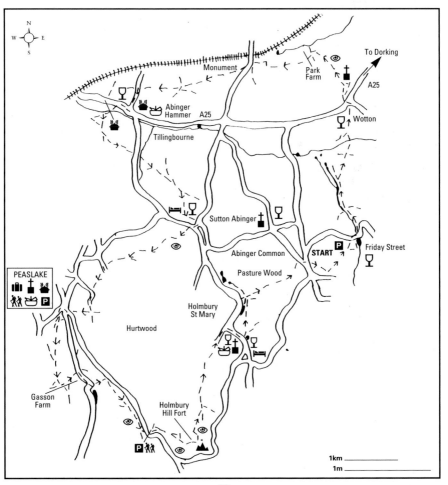

Walk Summary

This is a challenging but beautiful walk through some of the best countryside Surrey has to offer. It meets for a short period, three different walks from the original "10 Adventurous Walks in Surrey", but at the same time, explores a completely new part of the countryside. The going can be quite tough in places, with some of the paths quite muddy. However, the reward is glorious scenery and if you are lucky, a dazzling display by the local wildlife. If you are in danger of "dropping" en route, there are no less than seven hostelries where you can recover and bring some sincerity to the saying "for medicinal purposes only"!

Start - OS. 126457 Map 187

The walk starts from the public car park at Friday Street. To get there from the A25 or B2126, follow the signs to Friday Street. The car park is well signposted. Alternative starts can be made from Peaslake where there is a car park or from Hurtwood car park number one at Holmbury Hill (OS. 098432).

The nearest railway station is at Gomshall, from where you can walk along the A25 to join the walk at Abinger Hammer.

FRIDAY'S HURT

P From the car park, facing the road, make for the right hand corner of the car park to then follow a footpath which runs parallel to the road, going downhill. You will soon descend steps to meet another path onto which you should turn left and after a few paces, right to follow the road downhill to the Hammer Pond at Friday Street.

On reaching the pond, ignore a turning right and turn left instead onto a track, marked as a public footpath. Pass to the left of "Pond Cottage" and follow the track gently downhill to shortly cross a stream, via a small rickety wooden bridge. Thereafter, continue ahead until the track forks. Take the left hand fork to pass "Yew Tree Cottage" and carry straight on until you meet a gate beside a stile, with another stile on your right and on your left, a stone bridge which also acts as a dam. The bridge is a good if early opportunity to stop and enjoy your surroundings. Do not cross the bridge, but continue ahead to go over the stile and keep to a fenced track. The track follows the course of the stream on your left which descends by way of a series of minature weirs.

After approximately a quarter of a mile, the track forks and this time you should take the right hand fork (this is the first turning on the right since joining the track), to join a wide path now going uphill. The path at first runs between banks, which in wet weather help to turn it into a waterfall, before levelling out to cut across the corner of Damphurst Wood. Sometime on, go over a crossing track and carry straight on, now going downhill. The path soon levels out again but then descends steeply to arrive at a stile.

Cross the stile, thereby leaving the wood and continue along a fenced path between fields, descending the side of a shallow valley. Shortly after crossing the Tillingbourne, go over a stile and continue uphill through an old hazel coppice, to soon reach and cross a second stile which takes you into a playing field. Follow the left hand perimeter of the playing field ahead and on reaching a stile on your left, ignore this to bear gently right instead, still maintaining your route and making for a gate and stile ahead. As a guide, the gate and stile are sited between a village hall on the left and some houses on the right.

Go over the stile and continue ahead across a car park to reach a lane beside "The Wotton Hatch" pub, Fullers. Walk in front of the pub and cross the main road, the A25, to join a lane the other side signposted to Wotton church, St. John the Evangelist. Follow the lane to the church, ignoring a footpath off to the right on the way and take time to enjoy the magnificent views ahead of the southern escarpment of the North Downs. The tall church spire visible is that of St. Barnabas on the North Downs Way.

Wotton Church (OS. 126480 Map 187). *This unusual 13th century church has one of the best settings of any church in Surrey. Standing on high ground surrounded by fields with the North Downs as a backdrop, the church makes a fitting resting place for the diarist, John Evelyn. It was in this church Evelyn recalls, that he started his first lessons. They were conducted by a friar and were always held in the porch. Evelyn, along with three generations of his family, are buried at the church. A mausoleum to the north of the church lists the total eighteen Evelyn family members buried here.*

John Evelyn made it quite clear however, that he had no wish to be buried in the mausoleum and his tomb, along with that of his wife Mary, lie in the floor of the chapel. Before you leave the church, look for a set of eight heads carved above the south door. They are in fairly poor condition now but it is said that they once represented a priest, a baron, a king, a queen, a peasant, an archbishop (Stephan Langton), a pupal legate and a pope. If the interpretation is correct, it is the earliest known carving of a pope in England. Unfortunately, the church has recently been vandalised and therefore, you may find it locked.

Standing in front of the church gates, go over a stile on your left beside a farm gate into a field and follow a footpath which leads around the perimeter of the churchyard. On reaching another stile which leads into the churchyard itself, do not cross this but bear diagonally left to follow a prominent path across the centre of the field. At the far side, go over a stile and take a fenced path downhill, now following the perimeter of the field. As the field ends, ignore a path which leads off to the left through a thick hazel coppice and continue ahead through Deerleap Wood.

On nearing the other side of the wood, the path bends gently left and soon meets a stile which you should cross into a field. Continue in the same direction along a prominent path which crosses the left hand corner of the field and after passing over a ridge, descend to meet a junction of tracks in front of "Park Farmhouse" **(OS. 121484)**. Take the second track from the left which leads through the centre of the farm buildings, passing to the left of the farmhouse and thereafter, continue along the perimeter of Deerleap Wood. As you progress, the track narrows to form more a path and later bends right and then left to continue along the perimeter of the wood. Eventually, you will reach a lane onto which you should turn left and after approximately twenty metres, cross the lane to take a signposted public bridleway on the right. This is in the form of a track and runs through the wooded Abinger Roughs, soon marked by a National Trust sign.

Stay on the track, ignoring all turnings off, to shortly pass the derelict "Leasers Barn" on your right. Almost opposite this, look out for a large stone cross with an engraving of a walking stick and the letters "SW".

Samuel Wilberforce Memorial (OS. 111481 Map 187). *The stone cross marks the spot where Samuel Wilberforce, Bishop of Winchester, was killed on 19th July, 1873,* *after being thrown from his horse which stumbled over a rabbit hole. Wilberforce was on his way with Lord Granville to visit John Evelyn at Wotton, the purpose of the visit, it is said, to patch up an argument.*

At the time of Wilberforce's fatal fall, a shadowy figure supposedly his own ghost, was said to have been seen passing one of the windows at Evelyn's house at Wotton. Perhaps he was unhappy at being unable to settle their differences? The ghost is still said to haunt the house today as well as this spot.

Our route from the cross is straight on. However, if you are in need of an early rest, turning left takes you up a short ridge at the top of which is a conveniently situated bench and table, complete with view. As mentioned, from the cross follow the track until it eventually bends left in front of a field gate ahead. (Notice the carved tree stump along the way). Pass through the gate and continue ahead along the left hand perimeter of the field and at the far side, go through another gate to reach a track. Carry straight on along the track which runs through another wooded area belonging to the National Trust, known simply as The Rough. Ignore all turnings off and maintain your route, marked at regular intervals by posts with blue arrows. After a short distance the trees give way to a large grass clearing, a good opportunity to take a breather.

At the other side of the clearing you will meet a junction of tracks and bridleways. You should ignore all the turnings and continue ahead along the main track which, as before, is marked by the now familiar blue arrows on posts. The track eventually leaves the wood and runs between fields which are often grazed by Soay Sheep.

i   **The Soay Sheep** *comes from, as the name suggests, the island of Soay, part of the St. Kilder group of islands which in turn are part of the Outer Hebrides. The sheep is one of only a handful of breeds left in Britain that date from the Stone Age. In the Outer Hebrides they are still completely wild and are the only wild sheep left in Britain. They were brought to St. Kilder by the Vikings who used them for food as well as for their wool. They are still used for their wool today, which incidentally has to be plucked by hand, but their main use is in conservation. The Soay sheep are very light and are gentle grazers which make them ideal for grazing sensitive environments such as nature reserves.*

The track later arrives at a "T" junction in front of a field gate and beside it, a small wooden gate. Ignore tracks off to the left and right here and continue ahead through the small wooden gate and carry straight on thereafter, along the left hand perimeter of a field. To your right as you progress, apart from the North Downs, you can just see the rooftops and chimneys of the ancient "Packhurst Farm". At the far side of the field, pass through a small wooden gate to meet a lane onto which you should turn left. Follow the lane downhill to shortly arrive at a main road, the A25, in front of an antique shop at Abinger Hammer.

i   **Abinger Hammer (OS. 095475 Map 187)** *dissected by the A25 and the more attractive Tillingbourne river, is famous for its picturesque village clock. The clock errected in memory of Lord Farrer of "Abinger Hall", hangs precariously over the A25 with an iron worker striking the hour. It acts as an indicator to the importanceof the iron industry, once prevalent in this area. Today, the hammer ponds have been taken over by watercress beds. In summer, cricket is played on the cricket green beside the Tillingbourne and this can be a pleasant place to rest.*

For refreshments there is a small shop, a tea room which also serves good food and "The Abinger Arms" pub, Friary Meux. "The Abinger Arms" used to be a tannery before it started serving fine ales. It also serves food.

Cross the road with care and at the other side turn right to follow the A25 through the village and past a pond on your left. After passing an old shelter on the same side, take a track left signposted as a public bridleway and follow this past some houses on the right to shortly cross the Tillingbourne river. After the river the track, now concrete, bends right and shortly after, you should take a signposted bridleway off to the left. (Do not make the mistake of taking the bridleway ahead or the concrete track which carries straight on).

The bridleway leads gently uphill between hazel and holly lined banks, the foliage meeting overhead to almost form a tunnel. Ignore a stile and path on your right to soon after, go over a stile on your left, thereby leaving the bridleway to go into a field. Take care as this can be easily missed. Follow a prominent path diagonally right across the field to reach a stile at the far side. (If the field has recently been ploughed then use the trees at the centre of the field as a guide for which to head. There are four trees here, three close together on the left and one a little further over to the right. You should head for a gap between the trees on the left and on reaching these, bend left immediately after the tree on your left and head for the stile at the far side).

Go over the stile and take a path right which runs alongside a garden hedge, to shortly reach a track onto which you should turn left going downhill to meet a road, the B2126, or the Felday Road. Cross the road and go over a stile the other side. Thereafter, turn immediately right and follow the perimeter of a field, to meet and cross a stile and also a small stream by way of a wooden bridge. *In summer, the* *i* *sparkling waters below are home to the monkey flower, easily identified by its lush green leaves and bright yellow flowers. The plant was introduced to Britain in 1812 and became popular for garden ponds and streams. It quickly spread and today is quite common in the wild. The plant's native habitat is Alaska. Its name is taken from its yellow flower which is supposed to resemble a monkey's grinning face. I hope you have a good imagination!*

At the other side of the bridge, go over another stile and continue ahead along the right hand perimeter of a field, to ascend the other side of the valley. As you progress, ignore a stile on your right which leads into a wood owned by the Woodland Trust and carry straight on, still going uphill, to reach a stile. Cross the stile and continue across the centre of the next field following a line of telegraph poles. At the far side, pass through a gap in the hedge into another field and bear diagonally left across the field corner, still following the line of telegraph poles.

At the field end, turn right and follow the perimeter again keeping to the line of telegraph poles, and ignore a gap in the hedge on your left. The field perimeter soon bends left and at the same time, a bridleway joins your route from the left. You should ignore this and continue to follow the field perimeter, which after a few paces bends right. At this point, a path leads off to the left via a gap in the hedge. You should ignore this to still follow the field perimeter and telegraph poles and at the far corner, leave the field following the bridleway ahead which runs between banks. This soon leads out to a track onto which you should turn left. After a short distance, look out for a wooden gate on your right, which offers a lovely spot for a short rest and affords views across a valley to the hamlet of Sutton.

Stay on the track to shortly meet a lane where you should turn right to arrive at "The Volunteer", a Friary Meux pub. This is a lovely pub and popular with walkers, the terraced garden a delight in summer. The pub has recently started doing bed and breakfast and I can think of few prettier places to stay. From the pub, ignore another lane on the left and continue straight on to arrive at the B2126. Turn right along the B2126 and after approximately twenty metres, cross the road and join a path the other side, going up some steps to do so. The path which is fenced leads uphill between fields and climbs the other side of the valley. At the top it is worth stopping again to look back at the hamlet of Sutton and "The Volunteer" pub in its peaceful and welcoming setting.

The path leads to a lane in front of "Stile Cottage" where you should turn left to follow it for approximately twenty paces, before turning right to pass through some metal rails into a field. Continue straight on following a path along the right hand perimeter of the field, which runs between a fence on your right and some scrub on your left. At the far side, turn left onto a lane and follow this uphill between fields. As the fields end, ignore another lane off to the right opposite a plan of "Sutton Place" and immediately after, take an unmarked path right which runs behind some gardens on your right. This soon leads out to another lane where you should continue ahead, ignoring a lane off to the right.

On reaching the end of the lane carry straight on along a grass path between gardens, to shortly meet and cross a stile, thereafter following the path downhill. When the gardens on your left end, continue ahead along the right hand perimeter of a field still descending into a valley. Go up the other side of the valley to reach and cross a stile into a field, ignoring as you do so a path off to the left. Take a prominent path ahead across the centre of the field and at the far side, go over a stile and follow a narrow path ahead to shortly arrive at a concrete drive.

Follow the concrete drive which runs beside a market garden on your left until you meet a lane. Turn left along the lane to shortly meet a fork. Take the right hand fork and immediately after, ignore a footpath off to the right to carry straight on, along what is now a track. After passing a post box on your right you will arrive at a small group of houses, where you should ignore a track off to the left to continue ahead. The lane then ends in front of a wooden gate. Notice a house here on your left, "Rydings", which has a huge yew tree in its garden.

You should leave the lane here by passing through a gap beside a wooden gate and continue ahead along a narrow path, ignoring another path off to the left shortly after. The path soon leads to a tarmac lane onto which you should turn left. The lane runs downhill to shortly meet another lane beside a small parking area and a number of houses which make up the hamlet of Colman's Hill. Ignore a track on your left which leads to Hurtwood and join the lane on your right to follow it past a beautiful house on the right known as "The Southcots" (look out for the dragon on the roof). Pass another wing of the house "Woodcroft", after which the lane bends gently left to go uphill and soon arrives at a small gravel turning point beside another lovely cottage, where you should continue ahead passing through a gap beside a wooden gate. This takes you into Hurtwood where after approximately twentyfive metres, you will meet a prominent crossing path onto which you should turn right. After a few paces, this becomes fenced and runs between a field on your right and Hurtwood on your left. (Hurtwood - see "The Winterfold Wander").

The fenced path soon leads out to track where you should continue ahead. The track in turn graduates into a tarmac lane and as before, you should carry straight on until you meet another lane. Cross this and join a narrow path which runs steeply downhill and on meeting a third lane, turn right to arrive at the centre of Peaslake village, dominated by the "Hurtwood Inn", a THF pub and hotel.

Peaslake Village (OS. 087446 Map 187) *lies tucked away from the outside world amongst the lower slopes of Leith Hill. Its secluded position allowed it to remain for many years one of the last smuggling strongholds in Surrey. The church, built in 1829, is the daughter chruch of St. James' in Shere. Peaslake has always been associated with Quakers and has a Quaker cemetery situated south of the village. Many of the buildings are made of local stone and so blend neatly with the surrounding hills.*

At the village centre is "The Hurtwood Inn", an hotel named after the wood which encircles the village. The hotel which is THF owned, retains a good local atmosphere.

Peaslake Village
Stores

Sandwiches are served at the bar along with Courage beers and there is also a restaurant for those wanting more. The village also has a butchers (useful if you are camping) and a good general stores.

Cross the road ahead and follow it passing in front of "The Hurtwood Inn", ignoring just after a signposted public footpath off to the right. A couple of paces on take a signposted public bridleway on your left, which at first is in the form of a tarmac lane and leads up to the church, passing to the left of the village hall. Follow the lane behind the church and leave it to join a signposted public footpath ahead.

The footpath runs gently uphill and re-enters the beautiful Hurtwood. Sometime on, it passes a small parking area in front of the Quakers cemetery and continues ahead in the form of a track, now marked as a bridleway. This runs to the left of the cemetery, soon after which you should ignore another path off to your right. The sandy track now passes through a delightful area of ancient oak woodland, carpeted by the famous hurtleberries. After approximately a quarter of a mile, two tracks join from the right, beside a pine tree. You should ignore both tracks to continue ahead, thereby maintaining your route. As a guide, the wood has now changed from mainly oak to a mixture of silver birch and spruce.

Sometime on, the track forks and you should take the left hand fork, a track, to soon arrive at a track on your right and a footpath leading downhill on the left **(OS. 086437 Map 187)**. Leave the main track here and take the footpath left, going downhill along what is quite a steep path in places which runs between shallow banks. You will soon arrive at a "T" junction in the form of another path running between banks. Turn left here, still going downhill, where in wet weather the going can be extremely slippery and somewhat treacherous.

Further on, you will meet a track leading to a field gate on your right which you should ignore to continue downhill. Pass to the left of "Gasson Farm" and stay on the path which soon leads out to the farm entrance. Continue along the farm track to meet a road beside some cottages on your right. Turn right along the road passing in front of the cottages and follow it for a short distance, until it bends right in front of a drive to "Coverwood". Leave the road at this point and take a path left which leads uphill and passes a Hurtwood Control sign.

The ascent is a steep one and the tall pines appear to mock your slow progress. After what can seem an age the top is reached and at the same time, you will meet a crossing track. Turn right along the crossing track and after a few paces, turn right again to follow a track along the edge of the hill. The track meanders through more attractive woodland and you should ignore all minor turnings off. Sometime later, it narrows to become more a wide path and follows a fence on your right where the trees thin out to afford good views right to Pitch Hill. Sometime after, look out for a path forking off to the left which leads to a gate beside a green Hurtwood Control sign. Take this, thereby leaving the main track, (take care not to miss it), to after approximately forty metres, reach a lane.

Turn right along the lane and after approximately twenty paces, turn left to pass through a gate into Hurtwood Control car park, number one. A blue arrow marked with the letters "GW" indicates that you are now on the Greensand Way. Make for the right hand corner of the car park and just before this, take a narrow path right marked with a yellow arrow and the letters "GW", which immediately forks. Take the left hand fork, a narrow path, which soon descends the side of a bank to meet another path. Go straight across this and up some steps the other side to cross a newly created clearing with a pond on your left. Continue ahead along a narrow path which runs along the side of Holmbury Hill.

Sometime later, the path meets a grass path coming in from the left. You should bear right here, in the direction of the blue "GW" arrow and continue going gently uphill. After a short distance, this arrives at a wider path where you should bear right again, still in the direction of the blue "GW" arrow and continue to soon after, ignore a path coming in from the left. A few paces on, look out for a seat on your right recently errected, dedicated to "all free spirits" and in memory of Felix Laffan and Dave Birks, killed on the north face of the Matterhorn, July 1987. This thoughtful memorial allows you to enjoy some spectacular views in comfort. As you do so, spare a thought for all those who have died enjoying the great outdoors.

After the seat stay on the path, ignoring any further turnings off, to shortly pass through a series of banks and ditches, the olds ramparts of an iron age hill fort. You will then arrive at the top of Holmbury Hill with its stone memorial and recently built direction finder.

Holmbury Hill Fort 261m/855ft (OS. 104430 Map 187). *The stone memorial stands at the edge of Holmbury hill fort. From here there are excellent views across the Surrey Weald to the South Downs. Immediately below you is the village of Ewhurst, to your left (east) Leith Hill and to your right (west) Pitch Hill with, in the distance behind it, another hill fort at Hascombe and Blackdown. The views are in fact so good that it is possible to identify several of the walks featured in the Surrey and West Sussex "Adventurous Walks" series and will bring back fond or perhaps agonising memories.*

Holmbury fort is one of several hill forts built by the Celts along the Greensand Ridge. It is believed that their main purpose was not defence from each other but for combined defence again invaders from northern France. This form of defence existed right up until the second World War when the British army built similar defences along the North Downs.

Holmbury fort is fairly small compared to most other iron age hill forts. It is assumed therefore, that it was only lightly defended and doubled as a gathering place or somewhere to harbour animals. When it was built, the earth bank defences would have been strengthened with a wooden or stone wall. The banks which today are fairly unimpressive, would then have been tens of feet high and together with a deep ditch, formed a formidable barrier.

A favourite weapon of the Celts was the sling, particularly useful in fending off an attack on a fort. Amongst the Celts' prize spoils of war were their opponents heads which would be hacked from the bodies of their victims and errected on poles around the fort to warn off potential attackers. It is believed the heads of important enemies were preserved in cedar oil and kept at the Chieftain's house to be shown off to visitors.

After the Roman invasion, the Romans occupied many of the hill forts and there is evidence to suggest that this happened at Holmbury. The Romans slowly abandoned the hill forts as they built their own strongholds and although following their departure the Britons re-occupied many of them, it was only to be a temporary revival. The Saxons shunned them and the forts quickly fell out of use except as stockades for animals or as temporary refuges, somewhat ironic as this was probably one of the main purposes for which Holmbury was built.

To continue, keep to the Greensand Way by going straight across the hill top and take a path directly opposite, at the eastern side of the hill. The path leads downhill and soon bends gently left. It then leads along the side of Holmbury Hill with fantastic views right across to Leith Hill. You should ignore any minor turnings off to eventually, after much twisting and turning and more good views, meet a "T" junction in front of a post marked by a blue "GW" sign. Turn left here in the direction of the blue arrow and almost immediately after, ignore a grass path off to the right.

Continue to reach a grass clearing with a number of tracks leading off in various directions. Take the second turning from the right which immediately leads downhill and follow it to later meet a fork. The choice here is yours as both routes meet further on at a car park to the village hall at Holmbury St. Mary. Walk through the car park passing to the right of the village hall and join a lane which you should follow ahead to meet the first houses of the village. Keep to the lane to eventually meet the village green and more importantly, "The Royal Oak", Friary Meux. On the right, is the village church.

i

Holmbury St. Mary (OS. 110444 Map 187). *Before Victorian times, Holmbury St. Mary was virtually a wilderness well known for its smugglers and other inhabitants of dubious repute. The village, nestling in the shadow of Holmbury Hill, looks a lot older than it actually is. Nearly all the buildings visible today are Victorian, including the church which was built in 1873. Before the church was built the village was called Felday. Holmbury St. Mary was adopted upon completion of the new church. The village still has a small chapel with the name of Felday.*

"The Royal Oak" is popular and serves some good food, though if you want a good choice of real ale you should try "The Kings Head", a free house at the southern end of the village (ask a local).

Walk along the right hand side of the green passing in front of the pub, to meet the B2126 once more. Cross the road and turn right to follow it for approximately one hundred metres, where you should take a signposted public bridleway on your left. This is beside the old thatched village pump.

Follow the bridleway and pass through a small gate beside a larger one and continue, passing between a cottage on your left and a pond on your right. Soon after, the track forks and you should take the left fork, the less prominent of the two, which leads through picturesque woodland and becomes quite narrow in places. You should ignore all turnings off to later follow the bridleway behind some gardens on your left. The going can be particularly muddy even in dry weather, so I hope you are wearing those boots. After approximately a quarter of a mile, the bridleway meets a wide track joining from the left. As a guide, there is a gate and stile ahead of you here and another stile on your right.

Go over the stile on your right and follow a narrow path uphill which is quite steep at first and a test of your stamina after the miles so far completed. On nearing the top, the path widens into a grass track and cuts through the centre of Pasture Wood. Later, you should ignore a wide grass track off to the left and a narrow path on your right to carry straight on. Shortly after, the track descends into a dip where you should again ignore another track off to the right.

Sometime on, the track narrows to become more a path and at the same time, begins to descend and run between banks. It soon levels out to go over a muddy crossing track and almost immediately after, bends left to leave the wood and run between a field on your right and a large garden on your left. The path eventually leads to a lane and the southern tip of the hamlet of Abinger Common, marked by a small triangular green with a giant redwood tree and at one end the well preserved old village well.

i

Abinger Common (OS. 120455 Map 187) *is another Surrey hamlet hiding from the ravages of the 20th century. A house facing the well, "Goddards", was designed by that famous Surrey architect, Sir Edwin Lutyen. It was built in 1899 as a rest home for "ladies of small means" and was commissioned by the head of the Union Castle shipping line.*

A short detour left along the lane brings you to "The Abinger Hatch" pub, a free house. The pub consists of a huge flagstoned bar with a large open fire at its centre. The food is quite reasonable and there is a good choice of real ale. Do not be surprised to hear an Australian accent behind the bar.

Cross the lane and take a track ahead along the perimeter of the green and when after approximately thirty metres it bends left, leave it to take a narrow path ahead running across the corner of the green to meet another lane. Cross the lane and follow a path the other side across the wooded Abinger Common. After a short distance, the path forks and you should take the right hand fork which runs through quite dense woodland, particularly in summer.

Landmarks in a wood are difficult to describe, but at one point the path you are on does pass to the left of a large scotts pine which stands out from the rest. From here, the path becomes far more prominent following what is obviously an ancient track and soon after, passes some old brick foundations on the left. Further on, just after passing beneath some telegraph wires, you will meet a prominent crossing track onto which you should turn left, to pass through some beautiful oak woodland, the floor covered by the now familiar hurtleberries.

After a short distance, the track narrows to become a path and at the same time, begins to descend. Soon after, you should ignore a crossing path and carry straight on to meet a large junction of paths. From here, you have a choice of routes. The first is a direct route back to the car park (1), the second is via "The Stephan Langton" pub at Friday Street (2).

(1) If alcohol will only kill you off and all you want is to collapse into the comfort of your car, then from the junction take the second path on the left, (the path which forks left ahead), which runs in a straight line through some pretty oak woodland. It then bends right to pass between and follow a line of telegraph poles. You should ignore all turnings off and follow the path as it bends gently right to go between the telegraph poles again and continue to descend between banks and soon arrive at a lane. Go up some steps on your left here and retrace your steps to the car park, our starting point.

(2) If however, alcohol seems the perfect way to finish what I hope has been a perfect day, take the second path from the right (the path which forks right ahead), which takes you through more picturesque woodland, and continue to meet a crossing path in front of a scotts pine with telegraph wires attached. Go over the crossing path and continue ahead, passing to the left of the scotts pine and following a line of telegraph poles. The path winds downhill to eventually come out onto a narrow tarmac lane. Turn left here to shortly arrive at "The Stephan Langton" pub at Friday Street, where you can celebrate the finish of your walk with a well earned drink. To return to the car park, our starting point, follow the lane past the pub to reach a "T" junction beside the Hammer Pond. Turn left at the "T" junction and retrace your steps uphill to the car park.

If you have managed to visit all seven hostelries en route, then I recommend you do not drive home, but walk instead!

ACCOMMODATION

The Hurtwood Inn (THF), Peaslake. Tel: 0306 730851
On the walk, this is a friendly relaxed hotel at the centre of village life. The surrounding countryside is only paces from the front door, allowing for a pleasant stroll after the excesses of the evening.

The Volunteer, Sutton Abinger. Tel: 0306 730798
On the walk, this is an attractive and unspoilt country pub now offering bed and breakfast. Its setting is hard to beat.

Youth Hostel, Holmbury St. Mary. Tel: 0306 730777
Approximately one mile from the walk, this is a purpose built youth hostel set in large attractive grounds.

BUSBRIDGE OR BUST

Distance: 12½ miles (20.5 km)
Time: Allow approximately 6 hours
Map: Ordnance Survey Landranger Map 186

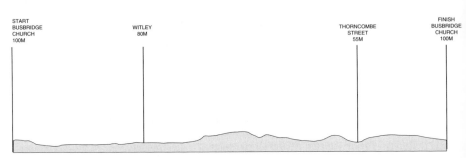

START
BUSBRIDGE
CHURCH
100M

WITLEY
80M

THORNCOMBE
STREET
55M

FINISH
BUSBRIDGE
CHURCH
100M

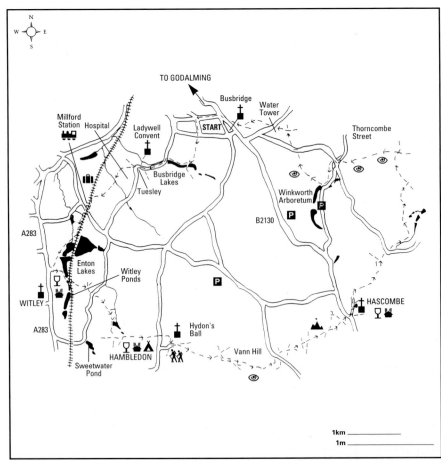

Walk Summary

Busbridge or Bust explores the beautiful rolling hills which escort the Greensand Ridge south of Godalming. The scenery changes quickly and almost every minute you find yourself discovering a new corner of Surrey. For much of the walk you follow that gem of long distance paths, the Greensand Way, with in places, glorious views across the Surrey Weald to the South Downs. Finally, this is not a route for coffee table walkers. Many of the paths can be very muddy and by the nature of your surroundings, there are several testing ascents. Wear those boots and ensure you are reasonably fit.

Start - OS. 978429 Map 186

The walk starts from the church of St. John the Baptist at Busbridge. To get there by car, if coming from the north, make your way to Godalming via the A3100 and from there, take the B2130 signposted to Cranleigh and Winkworth Arboretum. After a short distance, you will see the church on your right. A dead end road to the right of the church, Hambledon Road, has plenty of room for parking. From the south, join the B2130 from the A281 signposted to Godalming and continue for approximately six miles to reach the church which is on your left. Take a turning left immediately after the church and then left again to park in Hambledon Road.

There is a railway station at Godalming from where it is about a mile walk to the church at Busbridge. An alternative start can be made from Hambledon church (OS. 971390).

BUSBRIDGE OR BUST

From the church take a road left called The Drive which leads through and takes you past the smart houses of Busbridge. Pass St. Edmund's school and continue until you meet a crossroads where you should turn left onto Busbridge Lane. Walk to the end of the lane and cross a road ahead, to join a signposted public bridleway the other side. The bridleway at first, is fenced and after a short distance meets a crossing path. Go over this and carry straight on, the bridleway now lined by trees and running between fields.

The fields either side soon disappear and the bridleway then proceeds through a wood, where you should ignore all turnings off to now go downhill. As you near the bottom of a valley, your route will continue between stone walls and on your left through the trees, you will gain views across a beautiful lake. *This is Middle Lake, the middle lake of three. The lakes were created in the 18th century as part of the garden to "Busbridge Hall". The original hall was demolished, but the lakes and grounds along with several curiosities such as a hermits cave and a grotto, survive intact.*

Shortly after this you will meet a path on the right. Take this by passing through some wooden rails and follow a fence on your left protecting another lake, Lower Lake, to eventually meet a lane. Turn left along the lane and follow it as it almost immediately bends right to cross a stream which runs from the lakes just passed. As you continue, you should listen out for the chimes of a clock which belongs to Ladywell Convent, hidden behind trees beyond a bank on your right. *The name "Ladywell" is not as many think, a shortened version of "Our Lady's well", for the name appears to be much older than the convent. It is quite possible that the name could be of Celtic origin, as pools and wells (a well was usually a spring) were considered sacred.*

Sometime later, pass the grand "Tuesley Manor" with its ancient dovecote.

i **The dovecote** *was once a common sight in rural England and essential to the local economy. Today, they tend only to exist as a garden ornament or curio. It was the Romans who first farmed pigeons in a big way and introduced the practice to this country. After their departure, the art was forgotten until the Normans re-introduced it in the 11th century. Up until the 17th century, the privilege of keeping doves or pigeons was reserved for the landed gentry and certain sections of the Church. The poor peasant farmer not only had to survive by working a few acres of land, but would often have to sit and watch his master's pigeons fattening themselves for the dinner table on his hard grown crops. There were inevitably protests and eventually, the farming of doves or pigeons became a national right. With food, especially meat, in short supply, dovecote building became epidemic and by the end of the 17th century, it is estimated that there were over twentysix thousand of them in England alone.*

There were many attractions in keeping these birds. The lack of fodder to maintain larger animals through winter meant that most of them had to be slaughtered well before winter ended. Even if you were rich enough to keep animals through winter, it made for very hard work. There were no such problems with pigeons who basically looked after themselves. They also reproduced on a regular basis, guaranteeing a constant fresh source of meat and to compensate for their liking of the farmers' corn, their droppings were a valuable source of fertilizer.

The dovecote's end came with the introduction of root crops in the 18th century, which provided a cheap winter food source for the larger farm animals. A cow or pig went much further than a pigeon and did not ravage the crops and so dovecotes disappeared almost as quickly as they had arrived.

i Ignore a footpath off to the left opposite the manor and immediately after, ignore also another footpath off to the right. Keep to the lane to pass more beautiful properties which make up the hamlet of Tuesley, originally a Saxon settlement, its name derived from Tiw, the Saxon god of war. When the lane bends left take a signposted footpath on your right, going over a stile beside a gate to do so. Immediately after, turn left and go up a bank to join another signposted footpath, which can at times be somewhat hidden. This takes you onto a playing field belonging to Milford Hospital, where you should head diagonally right across the playing field, with the hospital buildings on your left. At the far side, bear left to follow the playing field perimeter.

Just before you reach an extension of the hospital ahead, leave the playing field and join a footpath which runs between hedges on your right, marked by a wooden post and a yellow arrow. The path quickly runs downhill between banks to cross a narrow stream and continues uphill the other side to meet the drive way to a cottage on your right. Carry straight on along the drive where there are good views left to a wooded hill top known as Hydon's Ball. The drive eventually arrives at a road beside Milford railway station and you should cross the road and turn right to cross the railway line and immediately after, take a signposted public footpath left.

The path, which is fenced, follows the railway line before bending right to pass through the centre of a wood. It soon crosses two streams, the second larger than the first, and later passes a large lake, Lower Enton Lake, part of Enton Lakes Trout Fishery. This is hidden behind a laurel hedge on your left. The footpath eventually leads to a track which you should join to continue straight on, to soon meet another track where as before, you should join it to continue ahead. Pass a house on your left, "Lakes Cottage", to meet a crossing track.

Go over the crossing track and join a fenced path the other side which runs between gardens and continue to pass a bowling green on your left, just before arriving at a narrow lane. As a guide, this is beside Witley Mens Club. *A short detour (half a mile) right and then left along the A283, will bring you to the historic "White Hart Hotel" at Witley, once frequented by George Elliot, where you can enjoy some early refreshment. You will have to retrace your steps to rejoin our route.*

The White Hart Hotel

If you are not in need of refreshments, turn left along the lane and follow it to soon reach the fairy tale "Enton Mill" and mill pond. Thereafter, continue to follow the lane under a railway bridge until you reach another small settlement known as Great Enton. Here the lane, now almost a track, reaches a "T" junction where you should turn right to pass in front of some outbuildings and then "Great Enton House".

Soon after, the track arrives at a lane. Cross the lane and join a signposted footpath the other side which leads up a bank to follow the line of a garden hedge on your right. After a short distance, this leads to a stile which you should cross, to follow a prominent path which cuts across the right hand corner of a field. At the far side, go through an old kissing gate and continue ahead, in the same direction, across the centre of the next field. The large building on the hill top ahead of you is a school.

Your route from here is downhill and at the far side of the field, you should cross a tarmac drive and then a stile ahead, ignoring a footpath off to the left as you do so. This takes you into a field where you should continue ahead along a prominent grass track to shortly pass a lone pond on your left **(OS. 958393)**. At the field end, pass through an old iron gate and follow a narrow path ahead through the beginnings of the wooded Buss's Common. Almost immediately after, the path forks and you should take the left hand fork, in the direction of a yellow arrow. Soon after, on meeting a crossing path, go over this and continue for a few paces to meet a wider crossing path, marked by a post and a number of yellow arrows.

Turn left here, where after a few paces you will meet another crossing path, which you should also cross. Immediately after, the path forks and you should take the left hand fork. After this, the path leads downhill to a muddy stream, often dried up in summer, which you should cross by way of a number of wooden planks to arrive at a bridleway the other side. Turn left along the bridleway through another area of mud, traversed in the worst place by more wooden planks, to soon bend right and follow the bridleway between fields. You should now stay on the bridleway to its end, a distance of approximately half a mile.

This takes you to the village of Hambledon where you will arrive at a road beside "The Merry Harriers", a free house introduced by a sign, "Open for warm beer and lousy food!". Contrary to its sign, I can recommend this establishment as being exactly the opposite and if you have time, I suggest you try what's on offer. If you feel you cannot go any further, the pub runs a small campsite on the green opposite.

Turn right along the road and then cross it in front of the pub to join a signposted public footpath opposite. Pass through a kissing gate and follow a narrow path gently uphill to later lead out onto a drive way. Carry straight on along the drive to soon arrive at a narrow lane. Turn left along the lane passing the beautiful "Court Farm" and thereafter, the picturesque St. Peter's church.

St. Peter's Church, Hambledon (OS. 971390 Map 186) *must be one of the most attractive in Surrey and with the collection of cottages that lead to it, creates a rural scene lost by so many of our villages.*

Strangely enough, although beautiful, it is not the church but the yew in the churchyard which attracts most attention. The yew is hollow and it is said that twelve people can hide in its trunk. If you have never seen a witch then walk around the tree three times and according to legend one should appear!

The lane ends beside the church and here the route forks, with a footpath leading left and a bridleway right. Our route is along the bridleway, the right hand fork, which is joined by passing through a small parking area belonging to the church. You are now following the Greensand Way. After the car park, the bridleway runs between fields where you are rewarded with views left to Hydon's Ball and beyond it to the left, the Hogs Back and Crooksbury Hill.

Sometime later, ignore a track off to the right leading to a reservoir and carry straight on keeping to the bridleway, to eventually arrive at a "T" junction in the form of a sandy track. Turn right along the track and after approximately twentyfive paces, take a narrow path left signposted as a public bridleway. Take care not to miss it. The bridleway runs up a bank and after a short distance, bends left to run along the edge of the Greensand Ridge, in this case Vann

Following the Greensand Way

Hill. It soon begins to descend the side of the hill and then forks, where you should take the left hand fork, thereby re-establishing your route along the edge of the hill. In places the trees on your right give way to afford stunning views south to the South Downs and in late summer, you are doubly rewarded by a rich feast of blackberries which line your route.

The bridleway takes an undulating route along the side of the hill and you should ignore all turnings off to eventually enter the corner of a field. Here you should continue in the same direction by bearing right along the right hand perimeter of the field, where to your left you will see a red brick tower which rises above the trees. This is the water tower at Munstead which stands only a few hundred metres from our starting point and therefore, a good guide as to how far we have come and perhaps more importantly, how far we still have to go.

At the far side of the field, pass through a gate and continue along the right hand perimeter of the next field and at the field end, maintain your route by following a prominent path ahead which leads into a sweet chestnut wood. Immediately after entering the wood, the path bends left and then right to run steeply downhill to meet a lane. Turn right along the lane for approximately twenty paces and then cross it to join a signposted public bridleway the other side, still marked as part of the Greensand Way (GW).

The bridleway runs gently uphill between banks and soon arrives at a gate through which you should pass, to continue your route ahead now following a much narrower path. The path continues uphill where, near the top, you will reach a crossing path. Ignore this and carry straight on along the bridleway which now runs in a straight line across the centre of The Hurtwood. Sometime on, go over a large crossing track and continue straight on through The Hurtwood and at a fork, keep left on the more prominent path and ignore all further turnings off to eventually reach a marked bridleway on your right, just before the path you are on begins to descend.

Turn right here in the direction of the Greensand Way arrow, where after a few paces you will meet a crossing path. Turn left along the crossing path, still part of the Greensand Way, and follow this steeply downhill between banks where shortly after, the path levels out to run along the side of a hill. Keep to the path until you meet another path, marked by a post and a yellow "GW" footpath arrow and take this to go steeply downhill.

Cross a stile into a field and continue ahead along the right hand perimeter, still going downhill albeit far more gently, and at the far side go over another stile. Walk across the centre of the next field heading for a gate and stile at the far side and far more inviting, "The White Horse" pub. Go over the stile and cross a road ahead, the B2130, to arrive at "The White Horse", a 16th century free house. The pub has an excellent reputation for food and in summer often has a barbeque which can be very popular.

From here, take a road to the left of the pub, Church Road, and follow this between rambling cottages to arrive at the centre of Hascombe village with its distinctive and ornate pond. A number of seats have been carefully placed around the pond offering an ideal picnic spot if the weather is fine.

Hascombe (OS. 002397 Map 186) *lies cut off from the outside world, its position on a dead end lane ensuring that time passes it by. Consequently, the village remains relatively unchanged and like all good villages, it has a thriving duck pond and some individual cottages. The church is the only fraud. Its appearance although ancient, is deliberately designed to mislead for the church was built in 1863. It cost £3,100 and is a wonderful example of what the Victorians could do to recreate an earlier style of building. One person of note who lived at Hascombe, was Nicholas Hussey, who was Sherriff of Surrey and Sussex during the reign of Henry VI whom he served.*

Follow the lane round to the left of the pond and stay on it as it bears left away from this tranquil setting. Ignore as you do so, a signposted public bridleway directly ahead. The lane leads past yet more perfect cottages to end at a gate beside another lovely cottage on your left. Carry straight on here, passing through a small bridleway gate and follow a tarmac drive to the left of a large house to join a wide path ahead, leading uphill through a wood. The going in places can be quite tough, especially if you have over-indulged at "The White Horse"!

On nearing the top go over a crossing track and follow the bridleway ahead to soon meet another wide track onto which you should turn left. Before doing so howevever, I recommend you stop for a breather and take time to enjoy the views back to your right over Hascombe village and the Greensand Ridge. Follow the track which immediately passes to the left of a barn which you will be glad to learn also marks the summit. It then leads away between fields to shortly re-enter woodland and sometime later meets a wide crossing track. You should ignore this and carry straight on along a track which quickly narrows to become more a path. It then runs downhill between banks with another path, also between banks, running parallel on your right. You will eventually arrive at a "T" junction in the form of a wider track.

Turn right at the "T" junction to continue your descent, though much more gradual here, to eventually arrive at a lane onto which you should turn right. Follow the lane for approximately thirty paces and then leave it to join a signposted public footpath on your left. This is just before a lovely old farm complex visible ahead. At first, the footpath leads through scrub and then meets and follows the line of a field on your left. When this ends, the path continues to follow the line of a second field on the same side, at the same time following the perimeter of an old chestnut coppice on your right, the floor of which is a maze of rabbit warrens.

The footpath eventually leads out into a field, where you should carry straight on along the left hand perimeter, also a grass track. There are good views as you walk, to your right across to Pitch Hill. At the far side of the field the track becomes more prominent and you should follow it until it bends right, where you should leave it to join another less prominent track on your left. This leads uphill following a fence on your left and shortly meets another track onto which you should turn left. After approximately ten paces, turn right and then immediately right again to descend open grass hillside. (Do not make the mistake of taking a track which runs along the perimeter of the wood on your left). The owners of the land to help walkers and to mark the Greensand Way, often mow the route of the path down the side of the hill. In case when you do this walk this is not so, there should as a guide, be a tennis court on your right and a house on your left. There are also lovely views ahead as you progress across to the North Downs.

Near the bottom of the hill the path meets a concrete drive onto which you should turn left. The drive soon ends in front of a small barn and you should carry straight on here, passing to the left of the barn and thereafter, continue ahead through a field, keeping to the right hand perimeter. Keep to the perimeter as it bends right to eventually meet and cross a stile beside a gate in front of a farmhouse.

Once over the stile you will meet a track onto which you should turn left, to later pass another attractive property on your right. Thereafter, keep to the track which now runs between fields. On reaching a point where there is a gate either side of the track, the track instantly narrows to become a path. You should ignore both gates and follow the path between banks to later meet a junction of paths, marked by a wooden post with several arrows (OS. 011424). Here we say goodbye to the Greensand Way by taking the first path left, marked by a yellow footpath arrow, which immediately enters a field.

Continue uphill along the right hand perimeter of the field with, as you progress, lovely views right over the house of "Thorncombe Park" and beyond, to Albury

Downs. On nearing the far side of the field, go over a stile on your right into another field and then turn immediately left to leave the field through a gap in the hedge. First though, it is worth stopping to admire the view back to Pitch Hill.

The path continues uphill through an area of newly planted woodland, after which it becomes fenced and follows a line of sweet chestnuts. The views here to your left, are across the Weald to the South Downs. You will eventually meet a large stile which you should cross to enter a field. Carry straight on along the right hand perimeter of the field to go over the top of the hill. As you progress, the brick water tower at Munstead will come into view, a clear indication and perhaps relief that you do not have too far to go.

As you approach the far side of the field and the western slope of the hill, there are more magnificent views. To your right up the valley is Guildford, directly ahead in the valley below nestles the hamlet of Thorncombe Street and to your left Hascombe Hill and The Hurtwood. The rich wooded area at the far side of the valley is Winkworth Arboretum, NT, something I recommend you take time at the end of the walk to visit before your journey home.

At the far side of the field go over a stile to immediately start your descent of the western slope of the hill, heading for the hamlet of Thorncombe Street. Your way down is along the right hand perimeter of the field where approximately half way down, you should look out for a wooden stile on your right. This is well hidden, so take great care not to miss it. Go over the stile to follow a narrow path between hedges which graduates into a track to eventually arrive at a lane beside a cottage on your right.

Turn left along the lane passing a craft shop in a cleverly constructed log cabin and just after this, take another lane right which is signposted to Godalming. The lane leads over a stream via a small brick bridge where immediately after, you should take a signposted public footpath left. This at first, follows a track before meeting a gate where you should cross a stile beside it, to enter a field. Once in the field, turn left and continue along the left hand perimeter to, after approximately fifty metres, cross a stile on your left and follow a narrow path through scrub. In summer, nettles can be prevalent here and protecting clothing (waterproof trousers), may be necessary.

After a short distance, go over another stile into another field, where you should continue ahead along the left hand perimeter. At the far side, pass a lovely barn, normally home to some noisy donkeys and cross a stile to carry straight on along the left hand perimeter of the next field. At the field end, cross yet another stile and follow a narrow path ahead which runs alongside a garage and soon arrives at a tarmac drive.

Turn right along the drive passing a pretty cottage on the right and just after this, if you look carefully through the bushes on your left, you will see a small lake which is part of Winkworth Arboretum. The drive now ends and you should follow a fenced path ahead to soon reach and cross a stile and enter a field on your right. (The path ahead before you enter the field, leads into Winkworth Arboretum). Once in the field, turn left to follow the left hand perimeter of the field and the perimeter of the arboretum, and at the field corner go over a stile and follow a narrow path ahead through woodland. You will almost immediately meet a crossing track which you should ignore to maintain your route ahead.

The path winds gently uphill and is well marked throughout. After passing over a track used to train horses, it becomes fenced and levels out to continue in a straight line to cross another horse track, immediately after which you should pass through a kissing gate onto a lane. Turn left along the lane and after approximately thirty metres, cross it to join a track the other side, marked as a public bridleway. This runs through a strip of woodland with enticing views through the trees on your right.

You will eventually meet a crossing path, also a bridleway, onto which you should turn left to now continue between gardens. This leads out to a lane beside the huge water tower of Munstead, now converted into a unique private residence. Turn left along the lane and after a few paces, cross the lane and join a fenced path the other side marked by a "No Horses" sign. From here on, you should be watchful for it was hereabouts not so long ago, that a local man claimed to have spotted the Surrey Puma!

The Surrey Puma is the name given to a fierce wild cat varying in description from a large domestic cat to a full grown puma. There are stories of such animals all over Britain, but apart from the famouse Beast of Exmoor, the Surrey Puma is probably the most well known and most regularly reported.

The first sightings started around 1960 near Farnham and then in 1964, a man picking blackberries at a spot very near to here, disturbed a cat-like creature which he claimed was at least three feet tall and five feet long. People investigating his claim later found a line of large paw prints nearby.

No matter how sceptical you are of such claims, it is interesting that no more than a mile away is a suburb of Godalming with the ancient name of Catteshall, which loosely translated means "hill of the wild cat"!

Perhaps now a little cautiously, depending upon your level of scepticism, you should follow the fenced path to later meet a track where you should continue ahead. After a short distance, the track becomes tarmacced and arrives at a "T" junction where you should turn right along a lane.

Follow the lane passing a number of attractive cottages including one with an interesting stone wall and tower, to eventually reach the B2130 beside Busbridge village hall. Turn right along the B2130 to shortly arrive at Busbridge parish church and our starting point. Before leaving it would be a shame not to have a look round the church.

St. John the Baptist, Busbridge (OS. 978429 Map 186) *is one of a number of churches built in the late 19th century by that famous Surrey architect, Sir Gilbert Scott (see "In Search of Lost Castles"). The most notable feature inside the church is the chancel screen which is the work of another famous Surrey architect, Sir Edwin Lutyens. Lutyens also designed the war memorial in the churchyard, something in which he specialised, his most famous being the Cenotaph at Whitehall.*

Buried in the churchyard is Miss Gertrude Jekyll who, apart from being an accomplished artist and writer, became famous for her work designing gardens. After inviting Lutyens to design her house at Munstead, they struck up a working relationship and a Lutyens house with a Jekyll garden was considered the "in thing" if you had the money. Fittingly, it was Lutyens who designed Miss Jekyll's elegant tomb.

ACCOMMODATION

The Kings Arms and Royal Hotel, Godalming. Tel: 0483 421545

Approximately one mile from the walk, this is a large historic hotel which has seen some distinguished guests. The rooms are well furnished and the hotel has a bar and restaurant which are both extremely comfortable.

The Pig and Whistle, Wormley. Tel: 0428 682362

Approximately one mile from the walk, this is a popular pub renowned for its food. The accommodation is comfortable and very reasonable. The added plus is that if you have no car, the pub is virtually next to the station at Wormley.

Youth Hostel, Hindhead YHA, Hindhead. Tel: 042860 4285

Approximately seven miles from the walk, this is a simple youth hostel situated in the bowl of the Devil's Punch Bowl. Basic but idyllic, I found it a welcome break from the 20th century. Camping is also permitted amongst the rabbits!

Camping and Caravanning, The Merry Harriers Pub, Hambledon. Tel: 0428 792883

On the walk, one can camp on a green opposite The Merry Harriers pub. What more can you want?

MONKS MADNESS

Distance: 13 miles (21 km)
Time: Allow approximately 6½ hours
Map: Ordnance Survey Landranger Map 186

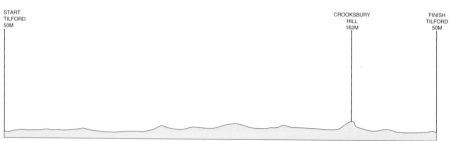

START
TILFORD
50M

CROOKSBURY
HILL
162M

FINISH
TILFORD
50M

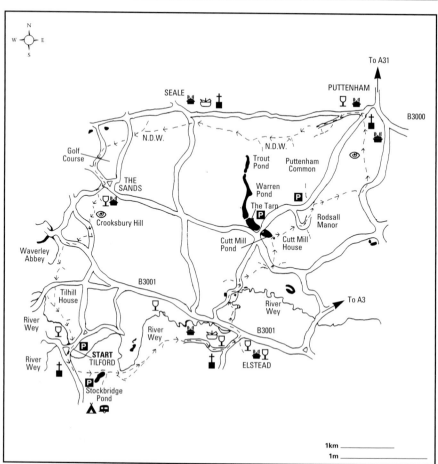

90

Walk Summary

This is a walk packed with interest. The route traverses some of the best heathland in Surrey and meets some historical villages along the way. In between, your eyes are drawn to a changing scene of rolling hills, haunting woodland, picture book houses and elegant lakes. As a finale, you climb Crooksbury Hill with a reward of the best views on the walk, before following the beautiful river Wey past the ruined Waverley Abbey, back to your starting point. The going can be quite muddy in places but in general the terrain is fairly easy. Do not though under estimate the distance, start this walk on a winter's afternoon and you will find yourself stumbling back in the dark!

Start - OS. 874434 Map 186

The walk starts at Tilford green where there is a small car park. To get there, Tilford is best approached by one of the two main roads, the A3 or the A31. From the A3, south of Guildford, take a turning signposted to Hurtmore, Charterhouse, Norney, Schackleford and Elstead and from there follow the signs to Elstead. Eventually, a fairly narrow road will take you to a "T" junction. Turn right and pass through Elstead and shortly after passing "The Donkey" pub, take a turning left, Green Lane, signposted to Tilford. After a short distance you will arrive at another "T" junction, where you should turn left and stay on the road to eventually arrive at Tilford green, which is reached by way of a small bridge over the river Wey.

From the A31, follow the main road to Farnham where you should join the B3001, signposted to Godalming. The B3001 passes Farnham railway station and after this, you should keep to the road, thereby leaving the B3001, which turns left here. Continue ignoring all other turnings off until you reach Tilford green. The car park is on your left at the far side of the green.

The nearest railway station is at Farnham. There is no obvious alternative start.

MONKS MADNESS

There can be few more lovely places from which to start a walk than Tilford green.

Tilford (OS. 874434 Map 186) *sits loosely around a triangular village green at the confluence of two branches of the river Wey. The green is approached by roads from three directions, two of which reach it by crossing over low stone bridges. Indeed, Tilford used to be more commonly known as Tilford Bridges. The bridges look old and so they are, built in the 13th century, probably by the monks of Waverley Abbey. There are well documented floods which occurred at the beginning of the 13th century and it is thought that the original bridges were swept away. Their replacements were built to last, though I doubt that their builders, even in their wildest dreams, realised that seven hundred years later they would still exist, carrying a much more destructive vehicle than the horse and cart for which they were designed. Today, the bridges are a popular place for families to gather and watch canoeists test their skills in the waters below.*

The green is also a cricket pitch and one with a distinct slope which has been cause for complaint by many an opposing team. The cricket club at Tilford has been famous ever since Silver Billy Beldham moved here in the 19th century. Billy was as well known in cricket circles as Ian Botham is today and once played for the famous Hambledon club in Hampshire. He was landlord of "The Barley Mow" which doubled as the cricket teams' club house and on retiring he moved to "Oak Cottage" next door, from where he could still easily enjoy the two great loves of his life, beer and cricket.

The pub has changed little since Silver Billy's day and is all the better for it. It is now a Courage house, which means reliable beer. Some good food is also served making it an ideal place to relax after your walk (not before!). At the rear, a pleasant garden stretches down to the river Wey. The pub also operates a tea room in summer.

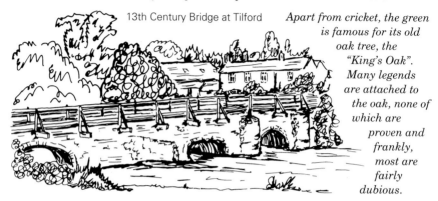

13th Century Bridge at Tilford

Apart from cricket, the green is famous for its old oak tree, the "King's Oak". Many legends are attached to the oak, none of which are proven and frankly, most are fairly dubious.

Tilford has several literary connections. Sir Arthur Conan Doyle (who also played cricket here), used Tilford in two of his novels and Sir J. M. Barrie used nearby Black Lake as the centre of "Never Never Land" in "Peter Pan". George Bernard Shaw was less impressed by the village and wrote with disdain of a ramble he took in the area, he also described Tilford as "a hole". Hopefully, you will not share his views - there is only one way to find out.

From the car park, facing the green, turn left along a road and follow it to the end of the green where you will meet a "T" junction. Turn left here in the direction of a sign for Thursley, Churt and Hindhead. To avoid road walking at this point, I recommend you take a fenced path to the left of the road, which is accessed by way of a metal gate. (If you wish to visit the church, then stay on the road for approximately thirty metres more to gain access. You will have to retrace your steps to rejoin our route). The church which is Victorian, is a good but ordinary example of its type. The best reason to visit is to purchase a booklet, "Tilford through the Ages", which documents Sir Bernard Shaw's account of his ramble and makes hilarious reading.

The path leads gently uphill with a field on your left and soon arrives at a wide track in front of a parking area. Pass through a metal gate here and turn left along the track in the direction of a red arrow marked with the letters "HR". The track follows the perimeter of Hankley Common and you should stay on it ignoring all turnings off, at one point passing a large house on your right, "Hankley Edge", to eventually reach Stockbridge Pond on your right and an army sign denoting an army training area.

Stockbridge Pond and Ice Houses. *The pond in winter used to provide Tilford with ice for its two ice houses. Ice houses were once fairly common and acted as giant communal freezers, essential before the invention of electricity. An ice house was constructed in a shady position around a well drained pit, which in winter would be packed with ice or snow. To further improve insulation a hedge or trees were planted around the building and the result was so effective that fish or meat could be stored safely for several months. Tilford's ice houses also, it is reported, served another purpose, that was to sober up drunks. I am sure ten minutes in an ice house would* *sober up the most dedicated drunk, these poor devils were locked up for the night and probably afterwards became strict teetotallers!*

Continue ahead passing to the left of the army sign and ignore any paths leading off to the right or around the pond. Pass another sign stating "Military Vehicles Only" and follow the track which bends right and then forks. Take the left hand fork in the direction of a blue arrow, still marked with the letters "HR", and continue to, after a short distance, arrive at an open grass area where a number of paths lead off in various directions. You should ignore all turnings off and carry straight on along the track, still following the blue arrow and "HR".

The track now runs along the northern edge of Hankley Common through silver birch and firs. As you progress, in places, you will enjoy lovely views left over the river Wey running directly below a sandy cliff. On meeting a fork, take the left hand fork, thereby continuing straight on and still following the blue arrows and "HR". You should continue your route ignoring any further turnings off, at one point passing an electricity pilon and later "Upper Hankley Cottage" on your left complete with tennis court, to eventually arrive at a large junction of tracks beside a small open grass area on the left. As a guide, a track leading left here is marked to "Hankley Farm".

As before, you should ignore all the turnings off and continue ahead along a track to soon arrive at a small parking area. Carry straight on, still ignoring any turnings off, and continue for approximately fifty metres to meet a lane **(OS. 896436)**. Turn left along the lane and follow it for approximately half a mile, passing on the way a number of picturesque farm buildings and crossing a pretty stream, to arrive at St. James' church at Elstead.

The Church of St. James' (OS. 904434 Map 186) *was built in the early part of the 12th century by the monks of Waverley Abbey. The abbey administered the church until the dissolution in 1536 of the monasteries, when it became a chapelry of Farnham. The church was heavily restored in 1845 and again in 1872, but has managed to retain its character. In the churchyard is a cedar of Lebanon, planted in 1849 in thanks that a devastating outbreak of cholera in the village had finally relented.*

Immediately after the church the lane forks in front of a small triangular green with a stone seat. You should take the left hand fork to arrive at a road onto which you should turn left. Follow the road, passing a cemetery and first World War memorial, to later arrive at Elstead village green.

Elstead (OS. 907437 Map 186) *struggles to retain its village identity as modern housing development threatens to turn it into a small town. The green although at the western end of the village, is effectively the village centre. It is also the most attractive part of the village. On one side of the green is the 17th century "Woolpack Inn", Friary Meux. Its name remembers the village's close connections with Godalming and the wool trade. The pub specialises in food and attracts people from miles around.*

Elstead has three more pubs. "The Star Inn", Courage, on the way to Godalming is the true village local and has an informal atmosphere. En route is "The Golden Fleece", Courage, (its name another reference to the once prosperous wool trade), which tends to be a bit upmarket. "Nellie Dene's", a free house, has taken over Elstead mill and is worth a visit if only to have a look, though you would be missing out if you did not sample the food. If you are on a budget, Elstead has a good fish and chip shop as well as a well stocked village stores.

Fork left at the green passing the village stores and continue to meet a road, the B3101, beside what was the old forge. Turn left along the road taking care of the traffic and pass "The Golden Fleece" to soon arrive at a small bridge which crosses the river Wey. *The bridge like those at Tilford was built in the 13th century, probably by the monks of Waverley Abbey. This one, unlike the Tilford bridges, has been heavily restored to cope with the traffic. The more modern bridge beside it was erected during the second World War and was only meant to be temporary, perhaps it too will survive seven hundred years? At the other side of the river, a sign advertises "Nellie Dene's" in Elstead mill. There has been a mill on this site since at least the 17th century and being so close to Godalming, it manufactured cloth and more recently, specialised in gold braid used on military officers' uniforms.*

Cross the road just before the bridge and continue along the pavement the other side to then cross the more modern bridge. At the other side, turn right and join a signposted public footpath which follows the course of the river Wey. The footpath follows the bank of the river for several hundred metres and then bends left to run between fields. On your left the other side of a field as you follow the footpath away from the river, you can just make out an old brick pill box, a reminder that the river was once part of a defensive line during the last World War (see "The Navigators Way).

After a short distance, go over a stile and continue ahead to cross a small bridge. Thereafter, cross two further bridges in quick succession, before once again meeting the river Wey. The footpath now follows the line of a garden on your right and continues to run behind some stables before meeting a stile. Go over the stile and follow a fenced path between houses and cross a second stile to meet a road. Turn right along the road and follow it, taking care of the traffic. *At the left hand side of the road are a number of large properties. One of them, "Fulbrook", had its own laundry which was later converted into a house and became the proud home of Peter Sellers and Britt Eckland and after them, Ringo Starr of Beatles fame.*

After approximately a third of a mile you will see a track on your right marked as a public bridleway and also as the entrance to "Broomfield Cottage". Take this and follow it until you meet a small wooden gate which leads into a field on your left. This is opposite a small grass clearing on your right, often used by locals as a parking area. Pass through the gate and bear diagonally right across a large field in the direction of a blue bridleway arrow. The way is quite undefined but as a guide, you will pass between a line of oak trees. Thereafter, you should head for three more oak trees in the distance, also in a line. As you approach these, make for a gate which is visible at the far side of the field.

Pass through the gate and follow a prominent and often very muddy path ahead through pleasant deciduous woodland, at one point going over a stream via a wooden bridge. The path leads to a lane where you should turn left to follow it for approximately thirty metres, before turning right onto a signposted public bridleway. This is immediately after the driveway to "Cuttmill Cottage". Follow the bridleway through more woodland, consisting mainly of silver birch, and continue to eventually meet and go over a crossing track. Almost immediately after, go over a bridge to arrive at the beautiful Cuttmill Pond, complete with fishing hut at the far side. *There is hardly a more tranquil scene in Surrey and yet the pond hides a dark secret. In 1932, the body of Albert Keen, a local man, was found in the pond. On visiting his home to break the news to his wife, the police found that she too had been murdered. Their killer and his motive remain a mystery to this day. The tragic couple are remembered by a plain gravestone in the churchyard at Puttenham.*

Continue ahead along a raised bank, a small dam, which runs between Cuttmill Pond and a smaller pond on your right and follow the perimeter of the pond, ignoring some steps on your right, to shortly arrive at the driveway to the rambling "Cuttmill House". Cross the drive and follow another drive ahead which follows a brick wall on the right and pass the pretty "Garden Cottage", obviously once the gardener's workshop.

After the cottage, the drive bends right and you should continue to follow it, still following the brick wall on the right. The drive leads to two more houses and here you should go straight on passing "Willow Cottage" on your right, to join a prominent path ahead, a bridleway. Go over a wooden bridge and follow the bridleway through attractive woodland, after which your route is between banks with fields either side to eventually arrive at a tarmac lane.

Turn right along the lane, ignore a signposted bridleway on the right and carry straight on to pass the beautiful "Rodswell Manor". After the manor house the drive ends and you should continue ahead along a track to pass two picturesque cottages. Almost immediately after, you will meet a fork where you should take the left hand fork, thereby continuing straight on, now walking between banks. The path runs gently uphill and further on you should ignore another path off to the left which leads up some steps. Approximately ten paces on, take a path right which is unmarked. Take care not to miss this as it can be somewhat hidden.

The path leads up the side of the bank, itself running between banks, to shortly pass through an area of young birch before arriving at a junction of paths. You should ignore all turnings off and continue straight on, passing to the left of a metal gate and following a path which is fenced on the right, in the direction of a yellow footpath arrow. The footpath leads gently downhill and later arrives at a large field. Pass through a gate here into the field and carry straight on, still going downhill, along the left hand perimeter of the field. There are views ahead now, across a shallow valley, to Priors Wood.

At the far side of the field, follow a grass track ahead for approximately ten paces to meet and cross a stile. Thereafter, follow a fenced path to meet and cross a second stile, before following another grass track ahead. Cross a wooden plank bridge and then yet another stile beside a gate, to arrive at a lane **(OS. 932463)**. Turn left along the lane and after approximately fifty metres, leave it to join a signposted public footpath on your left, going over a stile beside a gate to do so.

Go straight along the left hand perimeter of a field and when this opens out, bear left to continue following the field perimeter. The footpath now leads gently uphill to soon meet a stile which you should cross into another field. (Do not make the mistake of following a prominent path up a rise to your right). Go diagonally right across the field, which in summer is a mass of purple thistles, and go over a stile at the far side into the next field. It is worth taking time at this point to stop and look back at the views to Hindhead and Gibbet Hill.

Turn left along the field perimeter and continue to follow this round in the direction of the footpath arrows. On reaching the second corner of the field, go over two stiles in quick succession and follow a narrow fenced path ahead. Protective trousers may be necessary here in summer, when the nettles are particularly hazardous. After a short distance, you will arrive at a stile beside a derelict pergola on your right. Go over the stile and continue ahead following a track along the right hand perimeter of a field. Ahead to your right now is the magnificent "Puttenham Priory" and in front of you, the first houses of Puttenham, our next destination.

At the far side of the field, go over a stile beside a gate to meet a road. Carry straight on here passing the gates to "Puttenham Priory" on your right, to soon meet a "T" junction in front of the village pub, "The Good Intent", Courage, a warm welcome to Puttenham.

Puttenham (OS. 930478 Map 186) shelters in the shadow of the Hogs Back. On a rise at the eastern end of the village, sits a sturdy church which looks down a long street lined by a jumble of pretty cottages and houses. It is said that pilgrims once passed through Puttenham on their way to Canterbury. Today, the village welcomes a similar form of traveller, walkers doing the North Downs Way.

The church is essentially Norman, though the Victorians did their utmost to disguise this. The tower used to support a spire (the reason for its size), but this unfortunately was destroyed by fire in 1735. The village well in the churchyard is a recent and accidental discovery. In 1972, churchgoers arriving for the Palm Sunday service, were surprised (probably an understatement) to see a cyprus tree beside the path slowly disappear underground. A miracle? Unfortunately not, as unknowingly the tree had been planted on top of the village well, which had been filled in in 1750. The contents chose this opportune moment to subside, leading to the rediscovery of the well. The priory at the other side of the church wall is a fine palladin mansion dating from the 17th century.

"The Good Intent" is a good place to stop for a drink. Inside it has a pleasant mixture of old and new with several snug corners. The pub often has a selection of unusual guest beers and definitely recommended are the bar meals. It is a popular stop for walkers doing the North Downs Way so prepare to be humbled!

Cross the road and turn left to follow it past "The Good Intent" and through the village. When the road bends right beside the village stores, "Pilgrims News", leave it and carry straight on instead, along Lascombe Lane, in the direction of a North Downs Way sign. After a short distance, the lane forks and you should take the right hand fork, again in the direction of the North Downs Way, marked by a white acorn. The lane continues gently uphill running between banks and after approximately a quarter of a mile, meets some houses on your right. You should ignore a signposted footpath off to the left here and continue ahead, thereby leaving the lane, to follow a narrow path straight on which leads downhill.

On the North Downs Way

The path winds across Puttenham Common where there are good views right to the Hogs Back. It eventually forks in front of a Surrey County Council information sign for Puttenham Common. Take the right hand fork, still part of the North Downs Way and continue, ignoring another path which joins from the left soon after. You should maintain your route ahead to now go downhill.

Carry straight on, going downhill for some distance, until your route graduates into a track. You should ignore a turning off to the left here and continue ahead to soon arrive at a lane in front of a small brick bungalow. Turn left along the lane and after approximately ten paces, turn right, again following the signs for the North Downs Way, along a narrow path which runs between banks. After a short distance, you will meet and should cross a stile ahead beside a field on your left and thereafter, carry straight on along the perimeter of a new plantation on your right. Stay on the path to meet and cross another stile into a field.

Go straight on along the left hand perimeter of the field, with the field perimeter soon following the edge of a fir wood on your left, known as Payn's Firs. At the far side of the field, go over a stile on your left in the direction of the North Downs Way sign and follow a fenced path which runs between the wood on your left and another field on your right. When the field on your right ends the path then proceeds through the wood ahead and soon goes down a bank, bends right and continues between banks. Later the path forks and you should take the right hand fork to pass a large white house on your right before meeting a lane.

Turn right along the lane for approximately twentyfive paces and then cross it to join a signposted footpath the other side, still part of the North Downs Way. *A short detour by staying on the lane, will take you to the pretty village of Seale where apart from an interesting church, there is a craft complex which has a popular restaurant.* Our route however, is along the right hand perimeter of a field with views left across to Crooksbury Common, the centre of which is marked by an aerial mast. At the far side of the field go over a crossing track and carry straight on, now following the right hand perimeter of the next field. At the field end, follow the path as it twists right to enter another field and then immediately left to leave the field passing under an oak tree. You should now continue to follow a prominent path along the perimeter of a pine wood on your right.

After a short distance, the path you are on bends right and you should leave it at this point to continue ahead. A few paces on, go over a stile to meet another path onto which you should turn left, as before still following the North Downs Way. The path which is now fenced and lined by oaks, eventually arrives at a track which immediately forks. You should take the left hand fork to meet and cross a lane and join a prominent path the other side. Carry straight on following a fence on your right, behind which stands a smart white house. On your left are the grounds of Farnham Golf Club.

Stay on the path following the perimeter of the golf course and passing more grand properties on your right and follow it as it twists to arrive at a lane. Turn left along the lane, still in the direction of the North Downs Way, to soon pass a lone postbox (who uses it?). Sometime after, pass the golf clubhouse and continue to meet a "T" junction. Turn left at the "T" junction, thereby leaving the North Downs Way and follow the lane, later ignoring a road off to the right, Sands Close, to eventually arrive at a crossroads.

Turn right at the crossroads onto a lane called Botany Hill, in the direction of a sign to Waverley, Crooksbury and Tilford. If you are in need of refreshments however, then a short detour ahead at the crossroads for approximately fifty metres, will take you to "The Barley Mow" pub, Courage, an upmarket but friendly pub serving a good choice of food. Returning to our route, take the road right at the crossroads, marked as Botany Hill, and follow it until the houses on your left end. Here you

P should turn left into a small parking area and cross it to join a path at the left hand side, marked by a blue topped post and "P1".

Soon after joining, the path forks and you should take the right hand fork to follow a narrow path which winds through woodland. You should ignore all turnings off to shortly begin the steep ascent of Crooksbury Hill. When the path levels out it forks again and this time, either route is acceptable as they shortly meet at a "T" junction in the form of a wider path. Turn left at the "T" junction along a what is in fact a bridleway and when this forks (after approximately thirty paces), take the right hand and less prominent path to again go uphill. On nearing the top you will arrive at a "T" junction in the form of another narrow path. Turn right here to continue your route uphill.

The path becomes steeper as you go but you are soon rewarded as it suddenly leaves the tree cover to arrive at the open summit of Crooksbury Hill (163m/534ft), with superb views south. *A direction finder errected to T.V.C. Durant, once the Surrey Planning Officer, helps you to identify the main landmarks. Easily visible are Gibbet Hill, Beacon Hill, Butser Hill (directly ahead), King John's Hill and below to your right, the ruins of Waverley Abbey. The hill with its wooded slopes and bare top is in contrast to its appearance during the first World War, when all its trees were cut down, save a few at the summit. The effect was to create a startling landmark and Crooksbury Hill has been mentioned in travel books ever since, despite the return of its wooded cloak.*

From the top of the hill continue straight down the other side, which from the direction finder is in the direction of Broxhead Common. The way down is steep but the descent is eased by a number of steps. At the bottom of the hill you will meet a **P** parking area. Walk straight ahead through the car park ignoring all turnings off and follow a track the other side which shortly leads out to a road. Turn left along the road, taking heed of the traffic and after approximately one hundred metres at the point where the road begins to bend right, cross it and join a track the other side marked as a public bridleway.

The track passes a house on your left and then two pretty cottages on the right. It soon passes two more picturesque properties before winding through woodland to arrive at another road, the B3001. Turn right along the road, going downhill, for approximately one hundred metres and as the road bends right, cross it to join a track the other side. This is in front of a set of black and white arrows. If however, you wish to visit the ruined Waverley Abbey, detour by staying on the road for a short distance until you cross the river Wey beside an old mill pond, where the entrance to the abbey is on your left.

i **Waverley Abbey (OS. 867453 Map 186)** *is made for romantics. Set in a crook of the river its misty ruins watch over slow moving waters encircled in the east by an amphitheatre of tree clad slopes. The approach is equally dramatic, crossing an ancient bridge and treading a centuries old track beside a death-still lake and across fields grazed long before monks founded the abbey. The site was not just chosen for its dramatic setting, the rules of the Cistercian order which founded the abbey in 1128, the first in England, dictated that the abbey must be by a river and "remote from the conversation of men". Remote the site was as it still is today and nearby, a spring provided fresh water whilst the low hills on the far bank gave shelter from the north easterly winds.*

The ruined Waverley Abbey

It was just twelve monks who were sent from Normandy to found the abbey. This was another rule, all pioneering ventures to number the same as the Lord's disciples. One thing the monks had not bargained for was flooding and the building and even the very existence of the abbey, were severley threatened as the Wey burst its banks more than once during the 13th century. At one time, the flood was so devastating that the abbey was evacuated for several months and the monks moved to nearby convents to avoid starvation. If this was not enough, in 1215 their fresh water spring failed which threatened a year without wine. Typical of their spirit, one of the monks searched out another spring and brought its water to the abbey through pipes.

Although an important and very powerful abbey, because of its custom which forbade the monks in accumulating wealth, Waverley was also a poor abbey. Rulers of the land could not always distinguish between power and wealth and when King Richard I was held for ransom, abbeys around the country were ordered to surrender their riches to pay for his freedom. Waverley Abbey, living to its principles, had none and instead generously donated several bags of wool.

The honest reputation of the abbey meant that in later years it assumed another role. Aside of providing shelter for travellers, always a Christian duty, the abbey started to store peoples' belongings, becoming perhaps one of the country's first banks. Amongst the items deposited was treasure belonging to Aylmer of Valence, Bishop of Winchester, when he was forced to seek exile on the Continent. Henry III later abused the monks' hospitality by seizing the treasure.

The abbey in recognition of its importance, played host to several members of the country's royalty, despite their often ill treatment of the monks. King John stayed here in 1208 when the abbey was still being built and after him, Henry III. The monks probably sore at their rough treatment over the years, also welcomed Simon de Montfort and quietly supported him in his conflict with Henry III (see "In Search of Lost Castles"). The abbot for his disloyalty to the King on this occasion, was summoned to Parliament to explain himself but survived to return.

The uneasy relationship between the abbey and royal rulers finally came to a head in 1536, with the dissolution of the monasteries under Henry VIII. The abbot at Waverley made a valiant attempt to save the abbey by writing a passionate letter to Thomas Cromwell, who Henry VIII had placed in charge of the dissolution order. In his heart the abbot probably already knew that he could expect little mercy from a man who had so readily stepped into the executed More's shoes. Cromwell responded by making Waverley one of the first monastic establishments to be destroyed. Inside a month the monks were ruthlessly evicted, their glorious abbey being reduced to nothing more than an upmarket quarry.

Perhaps not surprisingly, living through so much drama, the abbey is reportedly haunted. The figure of a white monk it is said, can be seen searching the ground by night. Gory local superstition relates that the monk is one who was hung, drawn and quartered during the Reformation and is searching the ground for his entrails. I think we can safely assume that this tale probably started over several tankards of ale, perhaps at Tilford's "Barley Mow". Another local tale concerns the white witch of Waverley, Mother Ludlam, who was said to have lived in a cave, also the source of the original spring that served the abbey. The cave can be seen from the bridleway leading from the road the other side of the river, opposite the abbey's car park. The witch's cauldron is said to be the one in the church today at Frensham.

Returning to our route, the track which is fenced, runs through woodland and as you progress affords views right, where gaps in the trees allow, to "Waverley Abbey House" and the ruins of the abbey itself.

Sometime later the track bends gently left and soon after, you will meet a track off to the right, opposite a gate. Take this, at first going uphill between banks and keep to the track to eventually arrive at a lane opposite a stone barn with a postbox built onto the wall. Cross the lane and join a track the other side marked by a red arrow and continue for approximately twenty metres to meet a fork. Take the left hand fork to soon pass "Sheephatch Farmhouse" on your left and just after, a small white cottage on the right. Thereafter, the track narrows to become a path running between fields.

The path now runs gently downhill and sometime on, you should ignore a track which joins from the right. Continue ahead to eventually arrive at a tarmac lane which you should join to maintain your route straight on. You will soon pass "Tilhill House" on the left, complete with superb sculptured beech hedges. Just after this and opposite a white gate to another property on the left, take a signposted public bridleway right to run downhill with views over the river Wey on your right. Ignore a stile on the left.

The bridleway soon levels out and proceeds to follow the course of the river Wey which meanders through fields on your right. You should keep to the bridleway which in turn follows the river and ignore all turnings off to eventually arrive at a road and Tilford village. You will emerge beside the village stores and Post Office. Turn right along the road and go over one of Tilford's famous bridges, where the footway is still constructed from timber, to arrive back at Tilford green and our starting point. If you are in luck, you can end a perfect day by enjoying a drink whilst watching cricket on the green, or even the Morris dancers who frequently visit the pub. Your Good Health!

ACCOMMODATION

The Hogs Back Hotel, Seale. Tel: 0252 782345

Approximately half a mile from the walk, this is a large hotel adjacent to the A31. Primarily a business hotel, the facilities are excellent and a taste of luxury may be just what you need after a hard day's walking.

Little Cowdray Farm, Thursley. Tel: 0428 605016

Approximately three miles from the walk, this is a delightful place to stay. The farm is situated on an old drovers road south of Thursley. It is only a short walk to the National Trust owned Hindhead Common and not much further to The Three Horse Shoes pub at Thursley.

Youth Hostel, Hindhead YHA, Devil's Punch Bowl, Hindhead. Tel: 0428 734285

Approximately seven miles from the walk, this is a simple youth hostel situated in the bowl of the Devil's Punch Bowl. Basic but idyllic, I found my stay here a welcome break from the 20th century. Camping is also permitted amongst the rabbits!

Camping and Caravanning, Tilford Touring, Tilford. Tel: 025125 3296

Virtually on the walk, this site is in a particularly pleasant setting surrounded by Hankley Common, within walking distance of The Duke of Cambridge pub. The site is open all year round.

THE TOWER'S TERROR

Distance: 15 miles (24.14 km)
Time: Allow approximately 7 hours
Map: Ordnance Survey Landranger Map 187

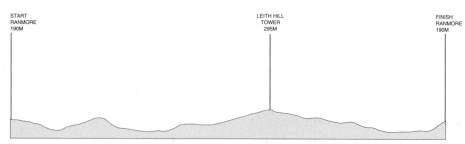

START
RANMORE
190M

LEITH HILL
TOWER
295M

FINISH
RANMORE
190M

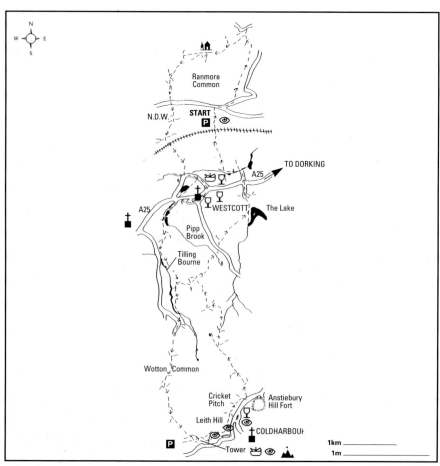

Walk Summary

This is the challenge walk of the book as not only is it the longest, but the route takes in some testing terrain exploring arguably the wildest parts of Surrey. From the heights of the North Downs the route traverses the beautiful Ranmore Common and then after a steep descent of the North Downs Escarpment, makes a slow gradual climb to Surrey's highest point, Leith Hill. After a lengthy descent of Leith Hill, the final test is a sharp climb to reach your starting point on the North Downs. If you are fit, the walk can be immensely satisfying and you will take pleasure in discovering some of the most remote and scenic countryside that Surrey has to offer. As always, mud can be a problem so wear those boots.

Start - OS. 143504 Map 187

The walk starts from the National Trust car park (pay and display) on the edge of Ranmore Common. If coming from London or the M25, take the A24 south towards Dorking and just before reaching Dorking, take a turning right signposted to Guildford. On meeting a mini roundabout, go straight across and at a "T" junction turn right. The car park is at the top of the hill on the left, shortly after two cottages on the same side.

If coming from the east or south, from the roundabout at Dorking where the A24 and A25 cross, take the A24 north towards Leatherhead. Turn left at the first set of traffic lights to reach the mini roundabout mentioned above. If coming from the west, take the A25 and just as you reach Dorking, turn left following the signs to Leatherhead and Ranmore. Look out for another turning on your left, Station Road, signposted to West Station, Ranmore and Effingham Business Park. Follow this road to the top of the hill where you will find the car park on your left.

Dorking has two railway stations close to the start, Dorking and Dorking West. An alternative start can be made from Coldharbour village.

THE TOWER'S TERROR

From the car park walk towards the road, cross it and then turn right along a wide grass verge. Follow this for approximately fifty metres, passing the "Old Post Office" and turn left onto another road signposted to Bookham and West Humble. Follow the road, also the North Downs Way, to shortly pass to the left of the church of St. Barnabas, also known as the "Church on the North Downs Way" or the "Walkers Church".

The Church on the North Downs Way (OS. 146505 Map 187) *is a valuable landmark for walkers for miles around. Its tall slender spire stretching up from the North Downs can be seen from most parts of Surrey and is a good bearing if you are lost on the maze of paths which cover Leith Hill. The church is a relatively recent addition to the downs, built by the famous Surrey architect, Sir Gilbert Scott, (see "In Search of Lost Castles"), in 1859. The church is considered to be his finest.*

The Church
on the
North Downs
Way

103

Just after the church and opposite the next building on your right, turn left onto a track signposted as a bridleway. The bridleway at first, leads past an attractive stone house and an equally attractive stone barn. Thereafter, it enters Ranmore Common proper, initially following the line of a field on your left. After the field, the track passes through the beautiful ancient oak woodland and scrub for which Ranmore Common is renowned, where as you progress, you should look out for fleeting glimpses of the abundance of wildlife that the common supports.

Stay on the track which descends gradually and ignore any minor turnings off to eventually, after approximately three quarters of a mile, emerge at the other side of the common. Here you should follow a fenced path between fields which descends into a beautiful valley. On nearing the bottom of the valley ignore a marked bridleway (which leads through a field gate on your left), and continue to take the second bridleway left which is just before a large white house, "Bagden Farm", visible ahead.

Pass through a small gate to follow the line of a low barn on your right and after passing through a second gate, take a prominent path ahead which follows the course of the valley. Sometime later, you will arrive at another gate through which you should pass to reach a well used track. Turn left along the track in the direction of the sign for the youth hostel and follow it gently uphill between banks and back towards Ranmore Common. As you progress, take time where gaps in the trees on your right allow, to enjoy views across the valley. At the other side of the valley, you may just see a long well trimmed hedge lined at intervals by statues. This marks the perimeter of the grounds of "Polesden Lacey House", National Trust.

The track eventually arrives at a beautiful small white cottage with an assault course in its grounds and in summer especially, a miscellany of tents camped in the woods around it. This is Tanners Hatch Youth Hostel, so appealing that it is difficult to resist knocking on the door to join the association! It is, in my opinion, one of the best and well run youth hostels in the south, where a number of popular events are held including the start/finish of mountain bike races, night hiking and a YHA-famous New Year's Eve party.

Walk past the youth hostel ignoring two tracks off to the left and continue to shortly arrive at a small parking area with a seat. Ignore another two tracks off to the left here and carry straight on, following an unmarked narrow path ahead. Go over a stile and continue ahead, once again passing through the magical woodland of Ranmore Common. After a short distance the woodland gives way to a field on your right with the early reward of lovely views across the valley to "Polesden Lacey House".

After the field, stay on the path, ignoring any minor turnings off, until you eventually reach and cross a wooden stile to meet a track. Turn left along the track and after a few paces go over another stile beside a gate. Pass a beautiful cottage on your right and follow the path ahead which now runs gently uphill, once again taking you back into the heart of Ranmore Common.

Keep to the path again ignoring all minor turnings off, to eventually reach a one bar gate with a magnificent beech tree on your right. Pass through a set of wooden rails beside the gate to arrive at a large grass clearing which has a National Trust "No Horses" sign. Walk straight across the clearing heading for a wooden fence directly ahead. Pass through the fencing and carry straight on to shortly pass through a gap beside another one bar gate, where you will immediately meet a prominent track.

Turn left along the track and after approximately twenty metres, turn right onto another track marked by a blue arrow. This runs parallel with the original track and after a few paces, meets another track which you should cross to continue ahead, still in the direction of the blue arrow. Stay on the track ignoring all turnings off to eventually arrive at a grass thoroughfare and the road which runs along the northern perimeter of Ranmore Common.

Cross the road where in the distance on your left, you will see the spire of St. Barnabas church passed at the beginning of the walk, and join a track the other side. Continue ahead along the track to soon pass a Forestry Commission sign, beneath which and mounted on an old tree trunk, is a sign denoting the Forestry Commission Bylaws. The track runs in a straight line through more woodland, where again you should ignore all turnings off. Sometime on, the track begins to descend and shortly after this, meets a crossing path marked by wooden rails, a yellow arrow and a white acorn, the latter indicating that this is part of the North Downs Way. It is also part of the walk, "All About Evelyn" in "10 Adventurous Walks in Surrey".

Do not join the crossing path but carry straight on, going downhill with the track appearing to descend forever (imagine doing it the other way around!). In places the going can be very steep and with a chalk base often treacherous, particularly in wet weather. On nearing the bottom of the hill ignore a path off to the left marked by a green arrow and continue to after a few paces more, arrive at a crossing track. Go straight over the crossing track and continue along a hedged path the other side, where there are good views ahead to Leith Hill in the distance.

You will soon arrive at the Guildford to Redhill railway line. Cross this, passing through a pair of white gates at either side and continue ahead along a track. When the track bends left, leave it and take a signposted footpath right which is quite hidden, especially in summer, so take care not to miss it. The path leads down a small bank through undergrowth and into a field, where you should turn left to follow the field perimeter and shortly pass over two small wooden plank bridges into another field. Carry straight on, still following the left hand field perimeter and when this bends sharp left, leave it to continue ahead now going across the centre of the field.

At the far side, pass through a gap in a hedge to enter Hurst Copse. Before this however, it is probably worth stopping for a short breather and to take in the views behind along the beautiful line of the North Downs. After entering the copse, the path immediately forks. Take the left hand fork, the more prominent path which meanders through the copse and at the other side, continue going downhill following the line of a field on your right.

At the far side of the field, go over a wooden bridge protected on either side by stiles and thereafter, bear left along the edge of another field to shortly go over a stile and meet Balchins Lane. From here, you have a choice of routes. If you wish to visit Westcott village with its attraction of three pubs, turn left. If not, turn right and follow the lane to reach the A25, where you should turn left for a few metres before crossing the road to rejoin our route at Rookery Drive (**OS. 134484**).

If you have turned left to visit Westcott, keep to the lane passing some lovely old properties, to eventually arrive at Westcott village green dominated by its well known thatched dovecote and bus shelter.

Westcott (OS. 142485 Map 187) *is a village that most people only see through their car windows from the A25. Seeing Westcott in this fashion however, means the real village is missed, for the best and prettiest parts are to be found along the narrow lanes which lead off the main road. Here you will find a jumbled collection of some of the best preserved homes in Surrey, many cleverly constructed with an eye to improving the landscape as opposed to destroying it.*

Along the main street, the A25, the walker has a choice of three pubs. At the eastern end of the village is "The Crown Inn", a free house. Outside hangs a blackboard on which, apart from the daily food specials, the landlord often headlines the village gossip. Inside, you can enjoy a lively but relaxed atmosphere. Opposite, is the "Prince of Wales", Fullers, which competes strongly for customers looking for food with its own blackboard. At the western edge of the village and en route, is "The Cricketers", a free house and a popular and relaxed local offering a good range of real ales. Facing the green there is also a general stores should you want to make the most of being outdoors.

The Dovecote on the village green.

Take the road right which runs along the edge of the green to shortly meet the A25. Turn right along the A25 and then cross it opposite "The Cricketers" pub, to join and follow a lane the other side which runs in front of the pub. Ignore a turning left, Heath Rise, marked as a public footpath and carry straight on along the lane heading for the village church. Enter the churchyard and follow the tarmacced path which passes to the front of the church. From the church porch you gain lovely views over Westcott to the North Downs. The church itself, like St. Barnabas, was built by Sir Gilbert Scott.

Pass the church entrance, ignore some steps on your right and follow a grass path ahead, which leads up through the churchyard to finally exit via a small gate. After the gate, turn immediately right and join a narrow path (if you reach a lane, you have missed the path right), to shortly meet a more prominent path onto which you should turn right. The path proceeds to cross Westcott Heath, running parallel with a narrow lane on your left serving some sleepy houses that overlook the heath. It soon meets the lane which you should cross to join a track ahead, marked as a public footpath and the Greensand Way, and also signposted to "Halcombe End". After a short distance, the track bends left to enter "Halcombe End". You should leave it here and carry straight on, going downhill, keeping to the signposted public footpath. The footpath descends through magical sandstone woodland and eventually arrives at Rookery Drive **(OS. 134484)**.

Turn left along the drive also marked as the Greensand Way and pass "Rookery Lodge". To your right runs the tiny Pipp Brook which once powered no less than six watermills. The drive leads past houses which could have been taken from a child's fairytale picture book, two of the prettiest being the "Mill House", which has a small waterfall adjacent and opposite, "Springs". Just after this and as the drive enters a private estate, "The Rookery", turn left onto a marked bridleway, also marked with the letters "GW", the Greensand Way.

The bridleway runs below a line of relatively modern houses on your right which eventually give way to a field. From here, we head back into the wild Surrey countryside. Further on you will arrive at a fork where you should take the right hand fork, a footpath and still part of the Greensand Way. This leads uphill through woodland and after a short distance between banks, affording the occasional good view left back towards the North Downs.

On nearing the top of the hill the path bends right to soon meet a track. Carry straight on here, in the direction of the yellow arrow and the sign for the Greensand Way, to after a few paces meet a more prominent track. Cross this and pass through a gap in the hedge the other side to enter a field and join a prominent path which runs ahead, bearing very gently diagonally left. This takes you across the right hand corner of the field. (If the path is unclear, then head for the wood the other side of the field, approximately fifty metres to the left of a cottage, visible ahead).

On reaching the far side, go over a stile to meet a track onto which you should turn left. Almost immediately after, ignore a marked footpath off to the right. The track goes gently downhill and after a short distance, runs behind some houses on your right. The going here can be extremely muddy and good walking boots or wellies are a must. You must now keep to the track, ignoring any turnings off, until it ends at a lane in front of "Triple Bar Riding Centre". As a guide, this is a distance of approximately one mile. Along the way the track takes you through one of the prettiest valleys in Surrey. Tree covered slopes border semi wild meadows, through the centre of which the young Tillingbourne stream descends via a series of small pools. Near to the track you will pass a number of man-made ponds, with the biggest and most pleasant surprise being a waterfall which cascades down stone steps into a deep black pool.

Turn left along the lane past the riding centre and ignore another track marked as a public bridleway on your left, to continue through the hamlet of Broadmoor consisting of a few sheltered cottages. The lane ends at "Whiteberry Cottage" and here you should carry straight on following a prominent path which is in fact, an unmarked bridleway. Ignore all turnings off and keep to bridleway which follows a line of telegraph poles along the bottom of a wooded valley, ascending gently. After approximately a third of a mile, the bridleway suddenly bends left to meet a prominent track. Turn right along the track, until after approximately fifty metres it bends sharp right, almost doing a "U" turn. Leave the track here and take a prominent path ahead and shortly after joining, ignore another path which forks off to the left.

The path continues ahead still going gently uphill along the base of the valley and you should follow it, ignoring all further turnings off, to eventually reach a junction of paths and tracks at a small clearing. As a guide, there is a one bar gate on your left here and a footpath sign. On the gate post is a carving of a dragon. Ignore all turnings off at the junction and carry straight on to follow a much wider track which continues through woodland, predominantly pine.

The track later forks and you should take the less prominent track, the left hand fork, now more a path. Take care not to miss it. This leads uphill through the pine wood, the sandstone floor either side of the path covered in summer by hurtleberries and bracken. On reaching a small area of open heather, ignore a crossing path and carry straight on, with a young birch plantation now on your right. The path meanders through a wooded part of Leith Hill, known as Wotton Common. *The origin of this path and many others like it was probably due to smugglers who found the woods welcome cover for their illegal activities. Until recently, many of the more prominent paths were still known as "brandy and silk" paths.*

On passing under a canopy of oak trees, ignore a path which descends on your left to a few paces on, meet another path onto which you should bear left. Shortly after, ignore a crossing path and continue ahead for a few paces to meet a more prominent path, where as before you should bear left to follow it. You will now be heading for the famous tower which sits at the summit of Leith Hill.

i

◉

▲

Leith Hill Tower 295m/965ft (OS. 139431 Map 187). *Leith Hill is the highest hill in Surrey. The tower at the top brings the total height to over 1000 feet above sea level, making Leith Hill, even if it is man-made, the only mountain in the south east of England. The tower was built in 1776 by Richard Hull who lived in "Leith Hill Place". Years later, during restoration works, his body was found bricked up inside the tower, this having been his dying wish. It is claimed that from the top of the tower you can see parts of thirteen counties (bring a telescope!), you can certainly spot the main landmarks of London.*

Despite its popularity, Leith Hill remains a wild place and there is no better time to visit than on a stormy day when with the lack of other visitors, one can really imagine Surrey as it was several hundred years ago. At the base of the tower is a small serving hatch where tickets are sold to visit the top, as well as light refreshments.

On reaching the tower, ignore a track off to the right and follow the main track around in the front of the tower and stay on the track, to descend in the direction of the signs to the Landslip Car Park. On arriving at a junction of tracks, take the second track from your right marked by a red arrow. This, as a guide, is the one after the track which descends between steep banks to your immediate right. The track you have joined goes gently uphill to soon fork and you should take the right hand fork in the direction of a red arrow and a wooden signpost, marked with a picture of a car and an "L" at the centre.

◉

◉

The track ascends to meet another junction of tracks. You should continue straight on to reach a one bar gate and a post with a green top, part of a National Trust trail. A short detour right here will lead you to a small view point. Our route however, is left after the one bar gate (do not go straight on in the direction of the sign marked by a car and the letter "L"), to follow a track along the crest of the hill where, in places, there are benches which allow you to enjoy yet more good views.

i

◉

Keep to the track along the hill escarpment and ignore all turnings off, including a wide track left opposite a bench. After this bench the track narrows and at the same time, begins to descend bending gently left. It then meanders around the wooded slopes of the hill following the green topped posts. As before, you should ignore all turnings off to eventually meet a wide track beside Coldharbour cricket pitch which is on your left. The cricket pitch is the highest in Surrey. Turn right along the track ignoring any turnings off and continue to descend into Coldharbour village. On your way you will pass a bench, carved from a tree which was blown down in the famous storm of 1987.

The track arrives at Coldharbour opposite "The Plough".

i

✝

▮

⌐

Coldharbour Village and Anstiebury Hill Fort (OS. 150440 Map 187).
Coldharbour, perched high on the side of Leith Hill, is the highest village in Surrey. Its setting is quite spectacular with just about every residence having a superb view across the Surrey Weald. Until late last century, Coldharbour was a dangerous place

renowned for smuggling. The wooded hills of this area known locally as Little Switzerland, were ideal for hiding contraband and yourself if the need arose - and it did! Often the smuggled merchandise would be buried safe from detection, the soft turf of the area making this option easiest and the most common. Occasionally, a local would stumble across such a hide and if this happened, he would mark certain items with a white cross and return them to their lair. The smuggler would then leave the marked items as a token of thanks for the silence of the finder. Apparently, the local villagers were sensible enough not to be too greedy.

Coldharbour and Leith Hill were also renowned for highwaymen and it is reported that at their height, even the greengrocer's cart carried a man armed with a blunderbuss. The tree lined hill behind "The Plough" pub is Anstiebury Hill fort, once an iron age fort and one of the largest in Surrey. The fort is 247m high and covers eleven acres. It was protected by a ring of three banks and ditches. The fort is still sometimes referred to as Danes fort or the Danish Camp, after a famous victory over the Danes led by King Ethelwulf in 852 AD. The Danes who were massacred are said to have sheltered at the hill fort on the eve of the battle. A large collection of human bones recently found on Leith Hill are believed to be their remains.

The fort was used again during the Napoleonic Wars to protect the women and children of Coldharbour from the long suffering and revengeful residents of Dorking, the smugglers' victims.

The church at Coldharbour is a relatively recent edition to the village, built in 1848 by one Benjamin Ferrey. For refreshments there is "The Plough", a free house (the highest pub in Surrey), which apart from serving some good food and interesting real ales, is one of only a handful of pubs in the county serving real cider.

As you enter Coldharbour do not join the road but turn left instead onto a track opposite "The Plough", to pass a Forestry Commission sign for Buryhill Woods and "Crockers Wood Cottages". The track passes to the right of some houses before heading into Buryhill Woods. It later passes an old loading platform on the left and soon after, meets a junction of tracks. Here you should carry straight on along the left hand track, passing to the left of a Forestry Commission sign for the protection of wildlife.

Keep to the track which at first leads uphill between banks and ignore two tracks off to the left beside a water tank to continue straight on. Ignore all further turnings off to the left or right and continue to eventually follow the perimeter of a field on your left, until you meet a pretty stone cottage on your right. Immediately after the cottage, turn right along another track and immediately after that, turn left onto a track which runs downhill into Squire's Great Wood.

The track descends without a break to eventually meet a wide gravel track. To your right hidden by trees is a small pond fed by a spring, known as Mag's Well. It was once believed to have medicinal powers and people from miles around came to be treated with its waters. Go over the wide gravel track to join another track ahead, still going downhill. The track soon bends left and levels out to pass through one of the remoter wooded parts surrounding Leith Hill. You should, as before, ignore all turnings off. Sometime later, the ground begins to drop steeply away to your right.

The track eventually ends at a "T" junction in the form of a more prominent track onto which you should turn left. Go uphill to shortly meet the wide gravel track onto which you should turn right, ignoring all turnings off. After passing a vehicle

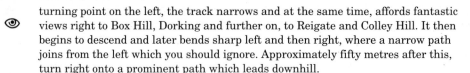

turning point on the left, the track narrows and at the same time, affords fantastic views right to Box Hill, Dorking and further on, to Reigate and Colley Hill. It then begins to descend and later bends sharp left and then right, where a narrow path joins from the left which you should ignore. Approximately fifty metres after this, turn right onto a prominent path which leads downhill.

After a few paces, you will meet another path onto which you should turn right to continue your route downhill, with a field on your right and a bank on the left. The path leads down to a gate through which you should pass to continue ahead along a semi-tarmacced lane. Stay on the lane, ignoring any turnings off, and pass a number of attractive properties to eventually meet another lane **(OS. 144473).** Turn left here and follow the lane for approximately ten paces before turning right onto a track, marked as a public footpath, and passing to the right of a house.

The track proceeds along the side of a hill with lovely views over the surrounding countryside to your right, spoilt only by two highrise buildings at Dorking. The footpath later forks and you should take the right hand path which leads downhill and follows the line of a field on your left. Pass over a wooden plank bridge to meet and cross a stile into a field. Continue in the same direction along the right hand perimeter of the field and on reaching the field corner, cross another stile to carry straight on, this time across the centre of a field.

At the far corner of the field, cross a wooden plank bridge and thereafter, a stile to follow a footpath left which skirts the perimeter of Bury Hill Fisheries, complete with well manicured lakes. The lakes are too artifical for my liking but one hopes that they will mellow with age, they are already attracting waterfowl. You will eventually cross a wooden footbridge over a pretty stream to reach a wide fenced path onto which you should turn left.

After a short distance, pass through a kissing gate to meet a lane beside "Keeper's Cottage". Carry straight on along the lane passing another house on your right, appropriately named "The Hedgerow". After this, ignore a signposted bridleway on the right and stay on the lane, ignoring any further turnings off and continue to pass more olde worlde properties to eventually meet the A25.

Cross the A25 with care and continue ahead along a track the other side, signposted as a public bridleway and marked as Lince Lane. Follow the track to its end where it bends left into the garden of a house and leave it to carry straight on along a narrow path to shortly reach and cross a small wooden footbridge over Pipp Brook. This leads you into a field where you are greeted by some familiar and magnificent views ahead of the line of the North Downs and the spire of St. Barnabas church at Ranmore.

Continue for approximately twenty paces along the perimeter of the field to reach and cross a stile on your left into another field. Go straight across the field following the brook on your left and at the far side, go over another stile and continue ahead along a narrow fenced path where after a short distance, you will meet two more stiles, one on your left and another ahead of you. Ignore these to turn right instead along a fenced path between fields heading for the North Downs and after a short distance, cross a stile to join a track ahead. It is worth taking time here for a breather and to look behind you, back over the village of Westcott.

The track soon leads to another track ahead which you should join to continue straight on, (do not turn right). You will eventually meet a stile beside a metal gate where a track joins on your right. Go over the stile and continue ahead along the right hand perimeter of a field. As a guide, across the field to your left now is a large white house, marked on the map as "Springfield". The way along the field perimeter is beautiful with a different view again of the North Downs escarpment.

Just before reaching the far side of the field, go over a stile on your right beside a metal gate and continue across the centre of the next field heading for a stile visible at the far side. Go over the stile and carry straight on across a third field, slowly beginning your ascent of the North Downs. At the far side of the field pass through a kissing gate and cross the Guildford to Redhill railway line once more and with care, and go through a second kissing gate to enter a field on the lower slopes of the North Downs, owned by the National Trust. Keep your eyes peeled here as this area is usually overrun by rabbits, who scatter in all directions upon your arrival!

Go straight across the centre of the field and at the far side go over a stile to enter a wood. Before doing so however, I suggest you again take a breather to prepare for your steep climb and enjoy the views back over Westcott, Leith Hill and Dorking. Follow the path uphill through the wood to later go up some steps and arrive at a crossing track. Unfortunately, we do not join the crossing track, but cross it to continue ahead, still going uphill!

At the far side of the wood, pass through a wooden gate to come out at open grass hillside. Ignore a marked path off to your right at this point and continue straight on up the side of the hill where, as you progress, fantastic views open out to your left. After what seems like an age, you will eventually arrive at the top of the hill where you may wish to stop for a well deserved rest. I have to admit that sitting here, despite the pain, is a marvellous way to end the walk.

To finish, continue straight on to reach and go over a stile to the car park, our starting point.

ACCOMMODATION

The White Horse (THF), Dorking. Tel: 0306 881138
Approximately one and a quarter miles from the walk, the hotel has a good restaurant and comfortable rooms, especially in the older parts of the building. At the rear there is a secluded open air swimming pool.

Crossways Farm, Abinger Hammer, Dorking. Tel: 0306 730173
Approximately two and a half miles from the walk, Crossways Farm is a Jacobean farmhouse, built in the early part of the 17th century. Its entrance is through a lovely walled garden up a stone flagged path. Inside, a great oak staircase leads up to comfortable rooms. If you wish to continue the magic of the olde worlde villages you have explored on the walk, then Crossways is a must.

Youth Hostel, Tanners Hatch YHA, Polesden Lacey, Dorking. Tel: 0372 52528
On the walk, Tanners Hatch is an isolated cottage (you can only reach it by foot). Situated in the woods of Ranmore Common, the hostel has no electricity so bring your own lighting. Camping is also permitted.

Camping, Polesden Lacey, Dorking. Tel: 0372 456844
Half a mile from the walk, this is a Camping and Caravanning Club site in a beautiful setting on an old cricket pitch in the grounds of Polesden Lacey, N.T. Please note, only tents and trailer tents are permitted.

SOME FURTHER
ADVENTURES

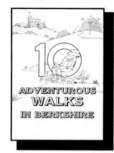

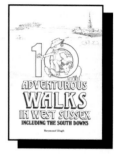

10
ADVENTUROUS
WALKS IN THE
SOUTH
CHILTERNS

10
ADVENTUROUS
WALKS IN
WEST KENT

KEEP UP TO DATE

If you would like a full list and to be kept updated on all the outdoor publications available from Morning Mist, please send a postcard with your name and address to Marketing, Morning Mist Publications, PO Box 108, Reigate, Surrey RH2 9YP.